MEXICO

HOUSES OF LOS CABOS

HOUSES OF LOS CABOS

AMAROMA EDICIONES

PROJECT EDITOR MAURICIO MARTÍNEZ ● PHOTOGRAPHY RIGOBERTO MORENO ● TEXTS FRANCISCO JAVIER IBARRA

HOUSES of LOS CABOS

PROJECT EDITOR
Mauricio Martínez

PHOTOGRAPHY
Rigoberto Moreno

SUPPLEMENTAL PHOTOGRAPHY
Rocío Guillén

RESEARCH
Francisco Javier Ibarra

ILLUSTRATION
Josel

TRANSLATION
Lucinda A. Mayo

EDITORIAL SUPERVISION
Augusta Cobar
Ángeles Fahara

TYPOGRAPHY
Ángeles Fahara

PRE-PRESS
Groppe

**DESIGN AND
EXECUTIVE PRODUCTION**
Amaroma Ediciones

AMAROMA EDICIONES
Av. Unión 266-302, Col. Americana, C.P. 44160
Guadalajara, Jalisco, México
Tel. 3616-5343. Fax 3616-5346
e-mail: amaroma@vinet.com.mx
amaromaediciones@yahoo.com.mx

English version: ISBN 968 5965-06-4
Spanish version: ISBN 968 5965-07-2

*PRINTED IN HONG KONG
BY GLOBAL INTERPRINT, INC.*

PROLOGUE

LOS CABOS,
A LIBERATED LAND

*T*he southern end of Baja California's peninsula has experienced such vigorous growth as to confirm its enormous development potential, its fate and mandate as a region whose incredible beauty, rich history and natural resources are still largely unknown.

In a geography whose inhabitants possess an innovative spirit, looking always to the four directions, Los Cabos' development reaches toward the shore, rapidly becoming an important and unprecedented force for social, economic and cultural progress.

New residents, new ideas and new lifestyles have all quickened the region's pace, highlighting the fragile equilibrium to be maintained in a serene haven whose natural history is measured in centuries.

The protagonists of this passionate, unprecedented and sometimes risky project face the enormous opportunity and responsibility of shaping enclosures to harmonize with their setting; to blend with the social fabric, and protect and preserve the natural heritage, which surround them.

Among the most attractive and fascinating aspects of Baja California's current development is definitely the visual impact provided by its new homes, where fine materials are used to express a convergence of diverse and lively influences – and where imported forms are increasingly giving way to the invention of a new Baja Californian architecture, with its own distinctive style.

It is an architecture flanked by the desert's rare and silent beauty, which looks out over the immense sea, with its fluid music and infinite shades of blue. The endless parade of homes is bedecked in warm colors, revealing the intensity of the sunlight in which each home basks, abandoning itself to its own dreams.

The fourth edition of Casas de Los Cabos aspires to be an ongoing and accurate witness to these happenings, and to this exciting chapter in modern Mexican architecture. A new collection of properties has thus been brought together; architectural works which testify to the wonders of Mexican construction and to the rich variety of designs and concepts employed in attaining the same goal: to build a home on the Baja California coast.

As in earlier editions, the book's purpose is handsomely served by Rigoberto Moreno's excellent and thoughtful photography, and Francisco Javier Ibarra's splendid prose.

Mauricio Martínez Rosas

Los Cabos, a liberated land

A beacon on the peninsula

Between the eternally, luminously blue sky and the wild waters of the Pacific Ocean and Sea of Cortés, Baja California Sur stretches alongside the northern part of Mexico like a land full of promises. Here it is possible to reach out and touch beauty, to feel the rough and varied splendor of the land; here, captivated by nature's mysteries, we can delve into a fascinating history and multi-faceted culture. Solving enigmas and finding new chances for growth, we can spend unforgettable holidays here, and make all manner of dreams come true.

Baja California Sur's origins go back to the Cenozoic Era when, following a series of powerful seismic shifts and a drop in the surface level of what are now the states of Sonora and Sinaloa, the peninsula began to pull away from the rest of Mexico's territory and to take on its own geographic traits.

After the violent creation of the Gulf of California – which from the seventeenth century onwards would be known as the Sea of Cortés – rough cliffs arose, and volcanoes, mountains and streams, strange plants to stand out against the desert plains that make up the terrain from Guerrero Negro to Cabo San Lucas.

Thus were shaped the landscape and climate that still color life in Baja California Sur: omnipresent heat that is barely dampened by summer rains or occasional tropical storms; cactus deserts that seem to brush up against infinity; mountain chains which make a dizzying descent to the sea by way of steep rock formations and rambling bays; expanses of desert populated by wind-tossed tumbleweeds, mezquite, saguaro and nopal cacti, *torotes* trees sand thistles; islands that can unequivocally be called paradises; waters where whales frolic and dolphins leap out of the sea – and from which fishermen haul quantities of tuna, abalone and clams; manta ray, shrimp and lobsters.

The first humans to inhabit Baja California Sur left their imprint here starting around 10,000 B.C. Discoveries of seashells, arrowheads, bones, skulls; hunting and fishing nets and wooden spears; palmleaf baskets, adornments fashioned of seeds and ochre-colored beads, among other material culture; signify that two primitive

cultural groups flourished here. One group occupied the central region and has been called the "Palm Culture"; the other, located in the northern region, is known as the "Comondú Culture".

Perhaps the most relevant ethnographic and artistic inheritance from these primitive communities is the collection of cave paintings, as mysterious as they are wild and lovely, which was created somewhere around 3,000 B.C., and which we can now contemplate in several caves along the San Francisco mountain range.

Halfway through the XVI century, when the first Spanish expeditions arrived, Baja California Sur was home to tribes which had developed from the abovementioned groups to acquire their own distinctive languages and cultures: the Cochimíes, Guaycuras and Pericúes.

Legends of *finis terrae*

Seduced by legendary tales that told of an island where women alone ruled over a land of gold and pearls, the Spanish conquerors headed by Hernán Cortés made several expeditions to the lands of Baja California Sur. In 1535, Cortés himself disembarked in what is now La Paz, and christened the port, "Land of the Holy Cross".

The first reference to the word California appears in the medieval epic poem, the *El cantar de Roldán*, written in France at the start of the XI century. This work, considered one of the pillars of French literature, mentions a land of marvels to the north of Africa, called Califerne, which was inhabited by stunning women.

Located by *El cantar de Roldán*'s anonymous author in the region of Berbería, the fortified city or "kalas" (source of the word Califa) was

inhabited by princesses and queens of the mythic Ben-Ifren, also known as the Kalas-Ifren, tribe.

Four centuries later, after discovering what is now America, Christopher Columbus decided to let his imagination soar once again, and in the detailed chronicle of his first trip to the Indies, referred for the first time to a fantastic western island occupied solely by women who were armed with bows and arrows, and who visited men two or three times a year to make love and be impregnated. The admiral preferred not to give directions to the so-called *Isla de las Mujeres*, Island of Women. In another travel journal five years later, Columbus mentioned sailing towards the West bound for this paradise on earth. Although the Genovese mariner didn't link the fabled Island of the Amazons with the alleged Eden, other expeditioners, seafarers and writers

would take it upon themselves to place the two in the same realm, and to employ all possible means for discovering that territory – an invention as heavenly as it was imaginary.

At the beginning of the XVI century, an alderman in the Spanish town of Medina del Campo who was also a writer of books on chivalry, was responsible for interweaving Christopher Columbus' charming tales with *El cantar de Roldán*'s exclusively feminine city of Californe. This novelist, Garci Rodríguez de Montalvo, entitled his chivalrous work *Las Sergas de Esplandián*, and it enjoyed great renown, popularity and credibility in its time.

The fifth volume in the famous saga of Amadis of Gaul, the book was first published in 1510 and widely read during the sixteenth and seventeenth centuries throughout Spain, Portual,

Italy, Germany, England and France. *Las Sergas de Esplandián* gave literary merit to the myth of California, surrounding it with a compelling, inspiring and legendary aura…

"Be it known that to the right hand side of the Indies there was an island called California, very near to being an earthly paradise, populated by black women, with nary a man amongst them, whose life was virtually that of Amazons. These women, true soldiers who adorned themselves with gold and pearls, loyally served Calafia, their queen…"

Twenty-three years after *Las Sergas de Esplandián*'s first edition, the Spanish adventurer Fortún Jiménez, who had never tired of poring through its pages, killed a fellow voyager named Becerra so that he might be the first to claim the fleeting glory of discovering, admiring and having

first set foot on Baja California soil. The thrill lasted only until the Spanish *conquistador* was killed by the region's bellicose tribes. Similar fates met the many would-be conquerors who followed, and similarly failed to tame the Baja peninsula's wild and restless beauty.

Ever since, this land's myths have been part of its fate: for nearly two centuries it was considered to be an island, if not a floating earthly paradise of indomitable women. And that despite the clearest indications by explorers, mapmakers, missionaries and other observant travelers that it was a peninsula, attached in the northwest to the territory of New Spain.

Over many years it was also believed that warrior women did exist here, attracting men with their charms like gorgeous sirens, then killing them after consummating the sex act in secluded

inlets, or in the vast lonely desert. When the infants were born, legend said, these women followed an implacable logic: if the child were male, he would be mercilessly put to death. Girls, however, would live to be educated and socialized according to the rules of this exotic female community.

Another legend that is still heard, especially in towns at the southern end of the Baja Californian peninsula, insists that those who eat plums from the Isla de Mogote, or taste the *damiana* flower, will not be able to leave the region alive, nor return to their place of origin. Instead, they will meet a woman who captivates them, and will be "condemned" to spend the rest of their days in the strange and ineffable paradise that is Baja California.

Even today, Baja California's myths, charms and seductions persist, against all odds: from Tijuana to Los Cabos, they lie beneath the surface of the region's economic, cultural and touristic development, surviving even modern social progress, with its various worries. Such legends, like Baja California's very name, are echoes of a fabled past emerging in the midst of its passionate, contradictory and problematic present.

A Union of Desert and Sea

There is no doubt that terrible battles took place up and down the Baja peninsula between indigenous tribes and Spanish invaders: gradually, the Europeans imposed a law based on their superior weaponry and technological knowledge. But the Spanish conquest was also a spiritual mandate, with the region's Jesuit and Franciscan missions playing an important role. The Jesuits remained in Baja California from 1683 when Father Eusebio Francisco Kino founded his first mission in La Paz, until 1768 when the order was banned from New Spain.

The Jesuits' tireless labor in founding a score of missions in Baja California Sur was continued by the Franciscans, led by Friar Junípero Serra. Both Jesuit and Franciscan architectural styles, as well as vestigial forms from ancient indigenous cultures, would influence the ways local identity was reflected in public and private buildings constructed along the Baja California peninsula.

Sparsely populated and isolated from the rest of Mexico, Baja California viewed the end of the Colonial era, the War of Independence and the national strife provoked by the Reform Laws from afar. It was wrapped up in its own struggles,

arising from the collapse and abandonment of old missions, attacks by pirates (their intentions as various as the flags they sailed under), and the gradual establishment of fisheries, of salt mining and exploration for metal ores.

In 1888 the peninsula was divided into two districts, and La Paz became the capital of Baja California Sur. Although the new constitutional designation improved trade and industry in the region somewhat, Baja California Sur in particular was fated to remain lightly populated, isolated and disconnected throughout the Porfirio Díaz regime, the Revolutionary era, and during most of the years that signaled Mexico's political, economic and socio-cultural modernization.

On February 7, 1931, the district of Baja California Sur became a federal territory: forty-three years later, on October 3, 1974, it gained its "free and sovereign" statehood. That brought Baja California Sur fully into contact with the rest of the country and the world, with ports being opened to development of its immense economic and touristic potential.

In the fifties, Mexican and foreign tourists began to be attracted by Baja California Sur's beautiful beaches, mysterious deserts and

venerable missions. But it was not until the seventies that the area truly took off as one of Mexico's principal deluxe tourist destinations; with construction of the transpeninsular highway, inauguration of the Loreto and San José del Cabo airports, the rise of high-quality hotels and resorts in the areas most visited, and creation of the Los Cabos-San José del Cabo and Loreto-Nepoló tourist corridors. Additionally, three areas were selected for developing tourism that would serve various markets: from Guerrero Negro to Ciudad Constitución, La Paz to Todos Santos, and from Los Barriles to Cabo San Lucas.

In Baja California Sur's recent unstoppable growth, public and private structures have played a major role. Particularly in the southern part of the state, they add an air of lasting sophistication, architectural elegance, sensibility and beauty to days and nights along the peninsula.

With their distinctive designs and dazzling style, their solutions for blending into the aesthetics of the landscape and their fascinating shadow-play, the best Baja California Sur homes offer us a chance to really view spaces and forms that have been created for their inhabitants' sheer enjoyment. They are another, perhaps more captivating, approach to gathering in the fruits of nature that grow in this liberated land, another way of understanding and enjoying these dream-like waters, prodigious deserts, underwater caverns; this endlessly blue sky, this vast paradise, this alliance and union that is Los Cabos, Baja California Sur.

Los Cabos' Passions

The rumbling sea crashes on the sandy beach. Waves ebb and flow in a rhythm that inspires meditation, contentment, being caught up in the moment. On one side, the sheltering sky stretches over the ochre shades of the desert; on the other, turquoise and emerald tides denote the immensity of the Pacific Ocean. In between, just a few meters from where sand dissolves into sea, there emerges a fantastic region which, like a beacon, allows us to glimpse and guess at the distance between known and unknown, to measure the magnitude of beauty that its light will reveal.

Like the antediluvian lighthouse facing the nearby mountain, which told the sailors, pirates and explorers of Baja California Sur's far west that they were coming to the end or beginning of the habitable world – a kind of *finis terrae* akin to that referred to in tales and maritime legends from the Romans, Celts, Portuguese navigators and Spanish conquerors – that is how Los Cabos appears on the horizon, imposing and alone.

Properly placed within the context of its surrounding geography, the Los Cabos region, with its own ineffable architectural style, respects nature's whims, and the massive neighboring mountains, fierce and innocent ocean, and signals from the old lighthouse that is part of its doting

view. In this sense, we can speak of Los Cabos as possessing an original kind of mirror-image or chameleon style, a style in which architectural elements try to respectfully reflect the principal features of their setting, so that they may thus dissolve and disguise temselves in the beauty of the landscape.

Along with that distinction, Los Cabos has another which has become a celebration of vitality, joy, sensuality and quality: it is the best example in Baja California of what a lively and light-filled community should be, with its homes open to the unfettered winds, desert echoes,

songs of the sea, friends' voices, and all the delights of the "good life".

Los Cabos is surely a unique beacon on the Baja California peninsula, a guide to the sense and sensuality of varied architectural solutions which incorporate the environment into an array of beautiful and functional, daring and discreet designs; all within thoughtful building plans. Los Cabos, with its unparalleled homes, is a beacon that lights the way so that we will never forget our return route to this corner of Baja California Sur, where the impetuous desert joins the impetuous sea.

Casa Estrellas

Architecture closer to heaven

Antonio Carrera, Architect
Jorge Carrera, Engineer
Grupo MCA
Architectural Design and Construction

Donn Bindler
Interior Design

F acing the Sea of Cortés' turquoise vastness, very near an island beach where old-time pirates here at the end of the world hid their treasure and their secrets, dominating the landscape with the elegance and force of an old sailing ship, between rocks and implacable desert, is Casa Estrellas, House of Stars: a home for contemplation, for living, for dreaming.

The sea inhabits this house day and night; a serene and peaceable sea that from time to time has its outbursts of temper. The Sea of Cortés literally embraces the residence, with its 240-degree panoramic view. From its lofty vantage point, like a seagull in full flight, Casa Estrellas fuses with the ocean and the desert, blends itself into its natural surroundings, their rhythms and fantasies, aiming to make this duet with nature its own symbol of architectural identity, its own privilege and treasure.

A ship smitten with the sea

Just as reaching this residence requires traversing several miles of winding road – among cactus, wildcats, squirrels, rabbits, roadrunners, *torotes* and *damiana* blooms – all in oppressive heat; so it requires we climb a number of meters up the desert mountain, the pirates' sacred mountain, to arrive at its threshold and prove ourselves worthy of the view that may be contemplated from the house's entrance area.

Passing through the property's long iron fence, at the same time that you observe passageways and roofs with the blue promise of the sea just glimpsed behind white walls, you also begin to descend by a flagstone ramp, lined in palm trees and leading to the rustic wooden front door. Before entering, you should amble along the outer walkway that encircles a good part of the house, a path with quarry stone

columns and a travertine marble floor inset with pebble mosaics. Under a roof woven of *palo de arco* or trumpet bush branches, you notice all around you the manifold greenery of this Mexican region; then a fountain that is a study of human face and features, followed by a series of distressed wooden doors that lead graciously to the guestrooms.

So near, yet so far

Architect Antonio Carrera confirms the challenge of building this house: "Brought to life on a spectacular lot facing the Sea of Cortés, this home was challenging for us mostly because of its remote location, and the lack of infrastructure and services around here. Still, the final result made all the trouble worthwhile. We decided to site the house up high, but then we had to do some banking of the land and build some retaining walls; always trying to downplay them visually, to blend them into the surroundings.

"The general concept of Casa Estrellas," architect Carrera continues, "consisted in integrating interior with exterior spaces, while subtly dividing off the guest area. Although sharing the same terrace, there's a virtual separation between the two spaces via a patio with a fireplace and pebble border. In this way, the family's children and guests can have more privacy, with their own pool, game room, and lounge areas. Or, they can join activities in the main area of the house.

Here, where the sea is a stone's throw away, so near and so far from each individual's musings, life alternates between private and communal, to the beat of waves and desert echoes; under an impressive floating ceiling that produces shade

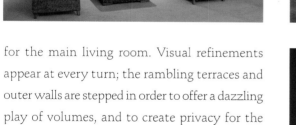

for the main living room. Visual refinements appear at every turn; the rambling terraces and outer walls are stepped in order to offer a dazzling play of volumes, and to create privacy for the spaces within and outside each bedroom.

. Casual, relaxed, functional, without any pretension beyond wanting to be a worthy and attractive home on the shore, Casa Estrellas extends an ongoing invitation to explore its mazes, to know the clarity of its architectural motivation, to tour its quiet rooms where – thanks to Donn Bindler's interior design – rustic and contemporary combine in a range of textures and colors that are always in balance. A

predominance of white makes for earnest elegance, and contrasts with the wood, stone and other natural materials of the region.

Stardust

Casa Estrellas' great luxuriousness lies not only in its striking paintings and graphic arts, with their frankly contemporary approach; nor in its chaise longues that evoke a relaxed mood and provide comfort; nor in the guestroom headboards, which transform the use of tile into a colorful puzzle-play. Nor is it only found in such details as the private fireplace in the gigantic master bedroom, the intricate passageways and terraces with quarry stone columns appearing here and there, or the palm-shaded jacuzzi that blends and dissolves into the sea's horizon. Nor is it exactly the bright kitchen, a wonder of functionalism and a magnet for gatherings; or the lamps which balance discreetly between living and dining room, with the gracefulness of dancers.

Casa Estrellas' luxury resides only partly in the stunning panoramic views that may be observed from each of its bedrooms the moment you enter them, from the terraces and many levels of the property, from the chaises, the game room, the garden that connects the house with the desert before bathing it in the ocean's waters. A view seen also from the infinitely enjoyable pool, from the kitchen and bathrooms, from the

bar and living room, from the exteriors lit to compete in majesty and mood with dawn or dusk, the first or last light of the day.

Actually, the house's greatest luxury has to do with the scintillations to which its name refers: the stars. There is nothing more intense, more gorgeous or mysterious, than contemplating the sky from this house, on a clear night or even on overcast one. Looking at the starry firmament, the purest and most lovely in Mexico, words fail and Casa Estrellas assumes its true dimensions: it is a private refuge, warm, intense, well-designed and beautifully-constructed, living under a sheltering sky.

Casa Brisa

A refreshing view

Jacinto Ávalos, Architect
ARCHITECTURAL DESIGN

Ávalos Arquitectos y Asociados, SC
CONSTRUCTION

From the first moment you set foot in some houses, and with every step you take, they literally astonish you with their enchantment and sorcery. They're not exactly haunted, but they do somehow seem to contain rambunctious beings from another dimension, who want to tour the house along with you. Full of light, with their openhearted architecture and their innovative style, still these houses provoke in their residents and visitors a feeling of being captivated and enthralled; constantly attracted, fascinated, mesmerized, we notice we're wearing our passions on our sleeve, and something's happening that makes us never want to leave.

Casa Brisa is one such place. As you move through the residential complex where this singular and incomparable house was built, and begin to walk towards the beach through a perfumed garden of chives and *damianas*, gardenias and jasmine, you encounter your first surprise – or, to put it another way you don't encounter but simply intuit the initial reason for your feeling of having been spellbound. The house you're planning to visit is beneath your feet! The grass

in this garden of a thousand scents is also the turf that covers the roof. To enter, then, you must put a little extra spring in your step and keep making your descent – while preparing yourself for other surprises you'll get, free-of-charge, when you reach and cross the magic threshold.

The eternal return

Casa Brisa was created with the intention of converting it into a kind of "wild card", with areas for multiple uses and events, within this small community between Cabo San Lucas and San José del Cabo. There are six other homes of similar dimensions, but none with the same captivating mystery as this one, which catches the breeze from the Sea of Cortés – the *orvalho,* as it is called in the *finis terrae* of Galicia and Spain.

Who would have thought that Casa Brisa would instead become, in the words of its owners, the real "trump card" here? Of course, the way it stands out from the other beach homes is not so terribly strange if we consider the building's history, and realize that architect Jacinto Ávalos viewed its design and construction as a kind of

adrenalin-producing gamble: "This house holds a lot of time, history, energy. For me it was always a challenge to bring all that to life. The goal was to see it through to its ultimate aesthetic consequences, and, as the satisfaction of the current owners confirms, I managed to achieve that. I needed to articulate and integrate the house with the residential setting and the beach, by making the building an extension of the garden, by giving the bedrooms function and flexibility, by presenting a great view of the sea – like a spectacular lookout point across the garden's green esplanade – and by building an entrance to the house that literally 'went through the roof'."

The foundation was set, platforms raised, and the house constructed in full hurricane season. Unable to wait for the weather to break because of budgetary and financing concerns, Casa Brisa overcame all obstacles along the way, beginning with gale-force winds, to become what it is now: one of the most outstanding, original, and self-assured beach houses on the Mexican Pacific coast.

The vibrant greens of Casa Brisa's rooftops compete with the watery blue echoes of the waves below – but there is no practical problem with dampness whatsoever. Architect Ávalos comments, "This type of turf roof is a good

example of putting appropriate humidity control into practice, beginning with a good foundation, reinforcing it with good structure, strengthening it with good banking of the land, protecting it with good waterproofing. We followed these methods step-by-step, and have had no trouble: just a very attractive aerial view from the top of the house."

After contemplating that cascade of green, you cross the fragrant garden and walk down the earth-toned access staircase, which gives you the feeling of scaling a canyon etched with cryptic symbols. Then you come to a patio built around a tree, a shady place to rest: it is a magical microclimate that signals you to stop, feel the quiet serenity of this space and time, notice how the colors of the house mimic the watery tones of the bay; to bask in the day's dazzling rays while listening to the rumble of centuries-old waves, to enjoy a bit of lightheadedness before entering a house that will invite you to become grounded in eternal mysteries.

Transitions and apparitions

Casa Brisa's eroticism is inseparable from its sensuous sightlines, room-to-room, and outwards into nature. Here in a wide-ranging and dream-like domestic design, the "unbearable lightness of being" becomes bearable. It is a space where everything flows without beginning or end, while its continuity creates unexpected reminders and reminiscenses of how natural and manmade volumes are interconnected.

A home for charm and enchantment at first sight: with the verdant firmament of the garden above the living and dining rooms, the skylights reflecting and refracting the sea's luminescence. The flow of air elicits sensations inspired by provocative crosswinds.

Granite supports the home's weightless spirit, quarry stone and travertine marble stretch the horizon. Windows seem to vanish, and great spaces open to display the immensity and radiance of the coast. Jalousied shutters make for warmhearted privacy; the patio lends intimacy to bedrooms which, if the occasion warrants, can transform themselves into parlors looking out onto paradise.

The pergola's liana columns contrast with the building's rationality; the height of each room creates a whole storm of proportions, but always brought back into human scale. Water used for irrigation on the grounds has been used and recycled by a state-of-the-art treatment plant. The edge of the pool draws the sea in, to create virtually another reality: splashing in the void, taking us by surprise, inevitably reminding us of the birth of Venus.

Casa Brisa is a prodigy of harmonious architecture, building and landscaping. Its lush earthy space, its liquid bubbling time, the circle of life between interior and exterior, its disguises and its deepest thoughts, all come together in a home that refreshes the eye with Los Cabos' endless variety of stone, sand, and waterborne dreams.

VILLA PEÑASCO

SERENITY ON THE CLIFFS

ALEJANDRO TREVIÑO ANGULO, ARCHITECT
CONSTRUCTION

TAPIA ARCHITECTS
ARCHITECTURAL DESIGN

FRANCISCO ROCHIN
PROJECT MANAGER

The gigantic and perilous rocks that edge the Pacific Coast along the Baja California peninsula create landscapes that are incredibly lovely, distinctive and unsettling, as the crashing waves of the planet's largest ocean meet the serpentine lines that define an oddly paradisiacal territory.

A place chiseled by time and nature, where countless interwoven elements bring an enigmatic land to life: desert textures, sparse and peculiar plants, towns and cities that have risen confidently despite all warning forecasts. Bays and seas with thousands of tales of pirates and phantom ships, marine species in danger of extinction and all sorts of spectacular rebirths, humans meeting inhuman challenges and surviving in solitude and exile, and men and women who avoid returning to their places of origin because they can't stop staring out upon this legendary horizon.

A few kilometers from where the Gulf of Cortés' waters meet the Pacific Ocean, among the most imposing cliffs in the Pedregal residential community, a structure seems to levitate to face the western waters, seems to be built upon those waters with no other purpose than to worship the Sun and Moon, seems to want to go beyond physical reality and blend with the spirits of darkness and light. This house pays homage to its name, as it stands, rock upon boulder upon craggy heights, to present itself as – Villa Peñasco.

From the heights

Starting at the entrance to this residence, wholly built upon a cliff around fifty meters above sea level, it becomes evident that the architectural tendency is to make sense and style of the home's different exterior and interior realms. This tendency is what we might call contemporary, but with some details, more than merely

decorative, which are circumscribed by the sphere of traditional architecture in this region of Mexico.

As a sample of what's in store when you pass through the large wooden door with its inserts of old ironwork and panes of iridescent stone: the façade's straight lines, uninterrupted by moldings, frame two waterfalls whose gentle liquid pounding reverberates in the entryway. On the upper level, a series of beams offers a welcome to this aerie; below, marble and flagstones have their turn to shine, while palm trees and rock gardens prepare our eyes to take in the exotic local vegetation.

"The most imposing challenge in this three-storey house was not drilling the rock to lay the foundation and create structure amidst wind and sea, nor even installing the elevator that carries residents from floor to floor. Without a doubt, the biggest complication was accurately interpreting the original architectural project and finding a happy medium, a point of equilibrium, for mixing contemporary elements with traditional ones, in just the right doses. I think it was sucessfully achieved because the owners, who had a very fine sense of their aesthetic demands, were completely satisfied and thoroughly contented – so much so that we have become excellent friends."

Waves over the boulders

Entering this incomparable clifftop house, after having inserted a smart card (just one of the technological complements to domestic life that emerge here and there) in the door, you may follow one of the two routes on offer: take the elevator and pass through the dual levels housing bedrooms, pools, passageways and gamerooms; or follow the path to a pair of living rooms – with their ceiling fixtures and indirect lighting, African masks and other pieces of ethnic and contemporary art – through to the dining room's fine woodwork and stained glass, aluminum juxtaposed against an openwork fiber rug; to the stainless steel kitchen and then, to the grand terrace where high-caliber glass banisters make the Pacific Ocean seem that much closer, fascinating and dizzying.

Villa Peñasco's walls are of glass – obsessively transparent, always challenging the eye with the dangers and attractions of the great ocean. The circular palapa with its furniture and its enormously-high-powered telescope, located on the terrace farthest from the home's massive signature boulder, almost seems to be an unidentified flying object: so suggestive and successful is the force-field at this end of the house. In its emptiness and fullness, the sea is drawn into blending with the property, reminding us with the liquid obduracy of its waves that it has been here for centuries. Onto the large terrace with its acid-washed marble floors and a pebble border that will accompany us everywhere we go on this tour, to the Venetian tile swimming pool that merges with the horizon and the merry waterfull inviting us to descend a staircase – which ends at the stepping stones of a reflecting

pool. Without a doubt, the traffic patterns of the built areas, which always take the cliff into account, are one of the architectural virtues and design qualities of this home.

At another level, the spacious and sensuous bedrooms: their baths with stylized grillwork open to the ocean, wicker furniture and glazed walls; their artful lines causing past and present to flow as one, stark ageless rock and hypermodernism, the showy curves of their walls and windows. This is also an ingenious curvature, allowing us to view the whole Los Cabos coast, from the Arch to Todos

Santos, to let our dreams and destinies travel the northern Pacific as far as the eye can see.

Villa Peñasco surprises not because its structure and construction are embedded in one of the most amazing cliffs in Los Cabos, nor because the captivating light of its interiors and exteriors shines upon an easy coexistence of traditional and contemporary, in this warm, fluid and ever-attentive setting. Below, the waves beat untiringly against the cliff face; above, night and day, life does a perpetual balancing act to imitate nature and art.

CASA SMITH

A FLAG FLYING IN THE WIND

JACINTO ÁVALOS, ARCHITECT
ARCHITECTURAL DESIGN

ÁVALOS ARQUITECTOS Y ASOCIADOS, SC
CONSTRUCTION

Ahome that is also a reflection, a song, an homage to a sincere friendship cultivated over many years. A home that is also an act of faith, a belief, a certainty transformed by trusting someone: to make an architectural project into a garden (a veritable garden of friendship) for mutual nurture, to trace out on paper the configuration of a space where one might live, love and dream.

Only from this lucid and affectionate perspective may one attempt to approach a full understanding of the marvel that is Casa Smith, that warm place that Susan Taylor and Micky Smith entrusted, with total confidence in his professionalism, design and structural talents, to Jacinto Ávalos: a house where a working relationship became a solid and resilient friendship, until Susan's recent death disrupted the trio's animated colloquy and led them along other paths. But the home remains: a wayside marker, a tribute, a trail of light facing the Pacific Ocean.

A magic door

Casa Smith has a very special energy. This has nothing to do with a warm feeling for some esoteric doctrine or pamphlet currently in fashion, but with an intimate reality. You need only arrive at its entry and observe its valiant attempt to display, as a testimony to this wild region's historic and biologic memory in a residential community, the largest possible array of indigenous vegetation. You need only see the red door with its little marine motifs, to know that you'are about to enter terrain that is liberated, and dedicated to pleasure and serenity; a reflection of space, passion and spiritual development.

A manifestation of professional capability and confidence (architect Ávalos says, "There is nothing more wondrous than a client, a 'patient' as I sometimes call them, who believes in you; and moreover, believes in you like a friend, unconditionally, loyally..."), Casa Smith is a space

charged with feelings and emotions which reflect the creative odyssey of an architect in the fullness of his growth.

According to Ávalos, "When I designed Casa Smith it was a time of experimentation and exploration, during which I was developing my own architectural theory. Because of that it is one of my most representative homes from that period. I was pretty anxious to achieve my own architectural style. Another thing is that I

wanted was to open up the vestibule, so that you wouldn't see the house right away when you entered, and the patio would be the center of the space. Now I'm glad to see that I succeeded in meeting that subtle challenge which so fascinated me: I emphasized the ocean views, blocked the sightlines to neighboring homes, transformed the patio and reflecting pool into an extension that would make the house even more open. By pure intuition I was exploring some

architectural ideas, some positions I held then, which brought me to a solution that's now characteristic of my work: exploiting the space so that people enter a house and come upon a grand esplanade that is also a social area."

Banner of friendship

If Casa Smith's exteriors present us with such wonders as the wild plum standing there like an ancestral presence, or the latticework that discreetly ensures privacy; in the interior Ávalos' aesthetic purpose was to unfold the space like a magic box with many tantalizing secrets: stone flooring evocative of Huichol Indian symbols, staircases leading to fantastic solaria, serpents pointing the way to the bedrooms, luminous circles for exchanging something more than experiences, sea urchins and starfish innocently stuck to doors, fish laughing around a reflecting pool that refreshes our whole outlook, a play of elevations and levels, the kitchen continually reinventing itself, cross-ventilation and infinite views across the the most extensive and intense ocean on the planet. Casa Smith is a genuine example of architectural intuitions and explorations brought to realization, to fullness, to radiance. It is

nothing more nor less than an architecture which may fearlessly eschew decoration to show its true self: a body to rise above the Pedregal, a spirit rooted in creating contemporary and minimalist solutions at the end of the world, a passionate subject and a time of gatherings under the banner of friendship.

That's why a flag waves from the home's highest, most central point: it flies for the mystery of creation, transformation's lights and shadows, wind in your face, the scent of night-blooming flowers, the sound of waves upon eternal rocks, the pure flow of space, the unfurling of any timeless banner. Casa Smith, like lifetime friends, in spite of all the changes, endures.

CASA GLORIOSA

A PLEASANT SOJOURN

ALEJANDRO ÁLVAREZ, ARCHITECT
BUCHAN HOMES
ARCHITECTURAL DESIGN

BUCHAN HOMES
CONSTRUCTION

BUCHAN INTERIORS
INTERIOR DESIGN

TROPICAL LANDSCAPE
GARDEN DESIGN

A residence created with the highest expectations for architectural design in a decidedly Californian manner; with budgetary freedom, many hours of creative effort, and plenty of "hard labor" on these rocks, with their dazzling panoramic view of the Sea of Cortés. Here in one of southern Baja California's most notable and exclusive residential communities, it would seem – theoretically and practically, ontologically and teleologically, because of free will and also determination – almost inevitable that a large house should be built.

In other words, Casa Gloriosa has risen to the challenge of its name, and the favorable circumstances of its birth – as a renovation project whose realization would leave no room for improvement. Then, the miracle of its growth, from the larval stage – simply wanting to build facing the Sea of Cortés – to the full-blown butterfly of its architectural proposal and present reality, which have established it as one of the most agreeable and pleasurable estates in the Palmilla complex, and in the entire Los Cabos region.

From *barranca* to garden

Casa Gloriosa's structural origins are the story of constant metamorphoses, the transformation of a wild canyon that flows to the sea through a garden of palm trees and *damiana* flowers, sheltering in its heart a cherished residence of light and passion. Time stops for a moment on its tiled rooftop, delights in the whitewashed tones of its archways, dissolves into the murmur of nearby waters; comes and goes, night and day, with the winds of chance over the voluptuous land.

Just so, the house glories in its own unpredictable ways: it swells with pride, floats along, fearlessly opens itself to all possibilities; evocative and provocative, it relaxes and excites body and soul until there is no recourse but to be led, seduced through its labyrinths indoors and out, its intensity and its secrets, its hidden corners and rooms designed for all the world to see. In this residence there is no more dignified and motivational task than that of giving oneself over to spatial and atmospheric freedom, to enjoyment and pleasure.

Walking through Casa Gloriosa means bravely entering a land of irresistible fascination. There may be no house with a more sensual ocean view in all of Los Cabos, nor any other house in all of Baja California with such dreamy, unselfconscious, refreshing eroticism.

But its sensuality is not a case of spontaneous generation, nor is it a product of calculated erotic intent. To the contrary: it derives from a particularly vivid and open-minded encounter between architectural elements and design, and an equable spirit that fills the senses "like water for chocolate" – not too little, not too much, not too cold, not too hot; "just right".

It's a space for running fingers over warm quarry stone and flower petals, listening to the murmur of water and birds in flight, smelling the enigmatic essences of its scented gardens, tasting the delicacies that issue from a kitchen where the cook is always ready to serve a full meal or savory snack, and contemplating a multitude of beautiful decorative details, from the bedrooms to a swimming pool that loses itself in the infinite horizon.

Enjoyment is destiny

The inevitable decision to transform the *barranca* into a garden, whether from a cosmological, constructive or perfectly playful perspective, led Casa Gloriosa on a quest for ways of showing the terrain to its best possible advantage: building platforms whose pyramidal form is softened by curving roofs and walls, making its stylized retention walls into little gardens for controlling erosion and displaying local flowers like *potentilla*, arranging its various solaria so that they appear at every elevation, from terrace almost to tideline. And, most fundamentally, arranging sightlines so that the Sea of Cortés appears from every area and through every window.

One characteristic that makes this home one-of-a-kind is its private beach. Thanks to the topography of the coast, to the cliffs that shield and watch over it from both sides and the ebb and flow of the tides, Casa Gloriosa has at its feet a small natural cove that bespeaks intimacy, that puts its finger to its lips and says "shhh...this is secret", that accentuates the house up above with all its vivacity and sensuality, its characteristic walkways and corridors, its columns and staircases, its rooms so perfectly interrelated with

the desert and seascape that can be observed through picture windows, from balconies, terraces and sun-dappled pergolas.

In summing up our walk through Casa Gloriosa's playful curves and pensive niches, an easy metaphor would be to conclude by saying that this residence is a glory, morning and night. But we can be clearer, more accurate than that: Casa Gloriosa is an treasure chest of subtle passions, a Baja California pyramid that attracts and liberates mystic and corporal energies; a scent, a caress, a look, an embrace. And, according to the creator of this voluptuous garden in a *barranca*, it is something even better: a pleasant sojourn.

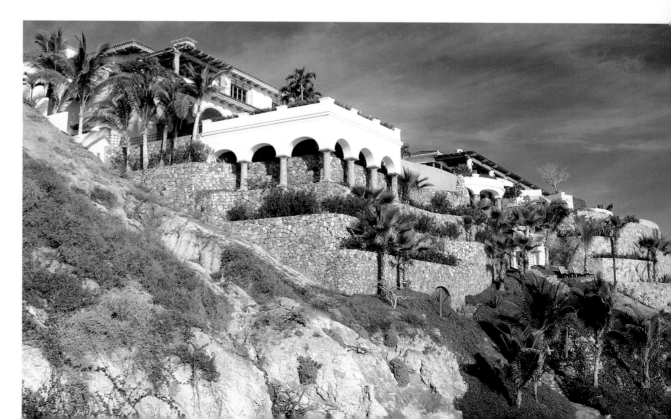

Casa Lorianna

Open desert, open sea

Stephen Berman, Architect
Architectural Design

Jaime Ortega Arnaiz, Architect
Homes at Cabo, S.C.
Construction

Casa Lorianna is an expression of the open sea, and the morning sun. Its stone terraces were designed to be part of the natural contours of the desert landscape, and its orientation is like an ancient Aztec calendar, with the rising of the sun and setting of the moon reflected in its central *palapa* on the longest and shortest days of the year. Could there be a more quintessentially Mexican beach house?"

The above words and poetic reflection by architect Stephen Berman, Casa Lorianna's designer, answer his final question: beyond symbolism and astronomical correspondences, beyond the blending of beach sands with those of the wild and ruthless Baja California desert, just a few kilometers from Cabo Pulmo, this structure borne of imagination and a wish to be useful, obstinate energy and plenty of heart, is an authentic beach home: perhaps the most deserving of that name, and the most relaxing, on all the península.

Unconstrained winds

To reach Casa Lorianna from Cabo San Lucas or San José del Cabo, one travels several kilometers in the direction of La Paz along a narrow highway and rugged paths: on each side, desolate lands with strange desert plants – mesquite and pipe organ cacti, *torote* trees, thorny thickets and tumbleweeds – stretch toward the hills and the sea. Along the way, a giant jackrabbit might cross your path, or coyotes, salamanders, chameleons, iguanas, roadrunners, quail, vultures, cardinals, coachwhip snakes, or rattlers.

As you step onto Baja California's warm desert sand, which will join the beach sand at the Sea of Cortés, your first views of Casa Lorianna appear: you immediately notice its symbiosis with the landscape, how it mimics the desert hills and sand dunes and seems to have been built without changing this chancy and chaotic geography in the least; and how it responds to any breeze or breath of fresh air with deepest gratitude.

Coming from the large free-standing garage, Casa Lorianna receives you with a sensual vignette: a cactus, a fountain, water flowing over stone walls and the desert buffeting your skin. Further on, once you've followed the sinuous lines of a welcoming path, a door opens onto a rotunda where a palm tree announces your arrival; then you walk out onto this dune which has become a house – the boldest, freshest, most original beach house in this region of Baja California.

Open to the cosmos

Casa Lorianna reveals itself as an abode with clear goals. It is a space designed to be shared; destined for relaxation, everyday private life, sociability at any hour, tranquility and playfulness, living between coloratura sunrises and sunsets worthy of Celtic lore.

Three large modules constitute this calm, uninhibited and restful residence: a large circular palapa, the master bedroom and two family and guest rooms. Each bedroom naturally has its own terrace, with lush vegetation and panoramic

views of the Sea of Cortés or the Baja California desert. These independent modules, whose curving walls, chromatic and formal finishes match the sand on the shore and the desert horizon, are connected by a terrace.

Is there any terrace more irreverent and irrepressible than this one, which looks out on the dancing emeralds and turquoises of the Gulf of Cortés? And encourages you to jump into the pool, swim a few laps or splash around, then run right down to become part of the beach?

Unpretentious and straightforward, Casa Lorianna is always making such sybaritic suggestions: to walk barefoot, smile upon your fellow man, shed any false rituals or apparel; to forget position and status, unbuckle egos and belts, "get naked" both spiritually and physically.

Here there is no other mandate than to be affable and lighthearted. Casa Lorianna will make sure you remember to be just a little mystical, and a little fanciful: to be your own woman, your own man, or maybe more; in a cosmos sizzling with fire and water, vibrating with serenity and turbulence, whispering with daily meditation and nightly passion, in this place between desert thorns and the ocean's redeeming waves.

Penthouse La Estancia

A step away from the Arch

Roberto Contreras Sandoval, Architect
Arkco
Architectural Design and Construction

Emma Laura Díaz Santana Rábago, Designer
Interior Design

Contemporary architecture has opened itself to many conceptual, stylistic and structural possibilities in our globalized; world ever-interconnected. The realm where spaces are created, at least, has continuously aimed to relate with all the rest of the globe – until it has reached a point of confusion and near-dissolution, a consummate stage where there exist a plethora of originals and copies, tendencies and identities from present and past, East and West; a straddling of modernity and tradition, public and private, individual and collective, sacred and profane.

In a post-modernist sense, this means that everything matters and nothing does: but new architectural and interior design currents have discovered ways of reevaluating eclecticism, creating a conjunction of styles and purposes from different eras and traditions through architectural projects that research the roots and consequences of any planned fusion. Without pretentiousness,

they seek also to consolidate and reflect the multicultural mix in new spatial realities; yielding designs that neither evoke nor invoke, but simply delve and confront, make sense of and amalgamate; constructing a new kind of pleasant and habitable setting.

To these structural and decorative tendencies, so counter to postmodern architecture, belongs the house set high atop the Hotel Villa La Estancia, just to one side of the geographic point symbolizing Mexico's authentic *finis terrae*; the Arch that embraces and intertwines the winds and waters of the Pacific Ocean and Sea of Cortés.

Medieval passion

Penthouse La Estancia is a design conceived and brought to life by architect Roberto Contreras, who was given absolute creative and inventive freedom by the client who hired him, trusted

him – and has been completely satisfied by the results of his intuitions, proposals and architectural quest.

As a starting point and guide to its meaning and layout, we can say that Penthouse La Estancia evolved from an intention to recreate its many rooms in medieval Tuscan style: heavy walls of ochre stone in the master bedroom and the great reception hall, marble columns, cupolas that inspire the sunlight to dance, marble floors composite, great exposed ceiling beams, murals and picturesque motifs scattered everywhere – bunches of grapes, bread, wine bottles, angels and cherubs, country women in rural scenery.

However, this medieval Tuscan theme is necessarily lightened by architectural and decorative counterpoints that treat the space to a blending of eras, cultures and traditions: a sensual Hindu sculpture in the entry hall separating Penthouse La Estancia from the rest of the hotel, behind a tempered bronze gate whose repeat image is a *fleur de lys*; a worn wooden door that also borrows esoteric imagery from the heart of India, with whirling suns and moons, planets and shooting stars; Moorish-style bronze grillwork in the bathrooms for privacy, but also to share the hallway's natural ventilation, and a modern terrace that wraps the living rooms in pale colors and minimalist lines, to complement the forms in the rest of Villa La Estancia.

If stylistic contrasts alleviate the heavy medieval Tuscan style of the Penthouse's principal areas, lending continuity to the entire residence, the conceptual and artistic quest of architect Roberto Contreras is also evident: "Architecture just impassions me. I love working in complete freedom, and doing an in-depth study for any project I'm on. After years in this field, I've hit upon a definition that works, at least for me: in architecture, you reach a point where all the design elements come together, leading anyone who enters the space you've created to really apprehend, with all their senses, what you wanted to transmit as an aesthetic, emotional and spatial experience. You start with a base for ideas, experiences, the architectural project and decorative goals, and then you work up to the apex of that pyramid. And when you get there, it's the space you dreamed of, intuited and created, as is the case with this Penthouse."

The ocean's angels

Wandering through this lofty residence, the sea seems to be always at arm's length – so close, that the boats departing from and returning to Los Cabos might sail onto the terrace and past the dining room (a jewel of clarity, quality and voluptuousness) before entering the living room. Here, where a painting of windswept women hides the television, above a fireplace reminiscent of a medieval castle, one perceives an intention to create unity amidst the diverse, though

predominantly Tuscan, stylistic tendencies – to give tangible shape to a space generated in the architect's desires and specifications, and above all in those of his aesthetic accomplice and traveling companion, the client.

Going past the gauzy curtains of the bedrooms, the offices with their equipment elegantly hidden behind bookcases and unexpected furniture, the soft curvature and lighting of cupolas and visual finishes, the art gallery on exhibit in the hall leading to the bedrooms..., we reach the place where Penthouse La Estancia really takes flight: the terrace. Here we are given a glimpse of the beloved and imposing Los Cabos Arch, and the waters that meet beneath it: waters of past and present, of memory and delight, waters from before time and those yet to be.

From the terrace of light and wind, nocturnal fires and endless conversations, spacious jacuzzi and *al fresco* meals; two angels witness as day becomes night, and rooms flow through Tuscan, medieval, Oriental, post-modern; their integral continuity lifting both resident and visitor atop a pyramid of dreams and aesthetic good intentions. The angels also bear witness to dawns and sunsets competing in beauty and boldness, to the rising of the tides, the growing severity of the gale, and the calming of the waters – reminding us again that the view is one divided in two , as in a garden with paths and destinies crossing – between nature in all its authenticity outside, and the delightful artifice within.

Casa Eichel

Landscape and art

Antonio Carrera, Architect
Jorge Carrera, Engineer
Grupo MCA
Architectural Design and Construction

Nanci Eichel, Design
Interior Design

Rising to challenges presented by the natural surroundings, achieving a spectacular panoramic view and fully integrating the qualities of the region's desert and seaside landscapes; these are some of the objectives of the great dream houses that are being constructed in Los Cabos to face either the Pacific Ocean or the Sea of Cortés.

Without discounting all the other work involved – the compositional and aesthetic sense, stylistic touches to the structures' interiors –; the concern with blending them into the landscape is surely one of the axes driving the vitality and "liveability" of these houses. The search for the best possible views of the desert – and optimally, of the sea – from every corner of these estates, is particularly evident.

In this sense, Casa Eichel is one of the most successful residences in this part of Baja California, since its will to style, architectural purpose and interior/exterior arrangements truly transfigure it, step-by-step, into a reverberation, a radiance, a mirror of time and space, and of the depth and beauty of Los Cabos' landscape.

Views *au naturel*

Located beside a beautifully laid-out golf course, within an exclusive residential community that lies along the corridor running back and forth between Cabo San Lucas and San José del Cabo, Casa Eichel gets our attention with its reserved dynamism, its affectionate lightheartedness, its capacity to invent and resolve space, its excellent siting at the highest point of a hill – where it perfectly captures a view of the bay.

Architect Antonio Carrera explains: "Building Casa Eichel on the highest and greenest lot in the development became a total challenge. But it was extremely important to us to set it upon a platform,

to heighten the possibilities for really suitable landscape architecture that would complement its great view over the Sea of Cortés. The idea that determined the façade's design was that the house should stand out in all its expansive magnificence, but the carport should be hidden; the leading visual protagonists would be the rocks, roof tiles and smooth walls that define the estate, inside and out."

Just as Casa Eichel's attractive façade glows with its own light, showing up splendidly against the playful luminescence of desert and sea as they're reflected in the features and the "feature stories" of this home, so another characteristic becomes evident from every angle: the exterior walls practically disappear from view, and one simply contemplates walls of greenery, with *huizaches* (acacias), saguaros and other cacti, *torotes*, *zalates* (wild fig trees), *damianas*, purple flowers, yellow flowers, mesquite, and wind-tossed tumbleweeds providing the most genuine solutions for continuity with Baja California's desert vegetation.

Exquisite artistry

Casa Eichel isn't just an impassioned testament to the landscape, searching out the most gorgeously bleak natural images in Punta Ballena from within the incomparable and ever-changing panoramic view of Los Cabos. Nor is it just the light of the house and shadows of its surroundings, or the perpetual play of outside illumination and interior penumbras.

On the contrary: just as the house blends perfectly with the manmade golf course as well as the natural exuberance of the region – where waves join forces with desert winds, and the jagged lines of the shore try to fit like puzzle-pieces into the craggy mountains – so in its interior rooms there pulses a spirit of "opposites attract", the interconnectedness of each one of its architectural, design and decorative elements as they fulfill their creative, imaginative and artistic purpose.

In exploring this home, we find ourselves everywhere confronted by an important work of art – on every wall, and tucked into every nook and cranny. Sculptures, paintings, graphic works, photographs, utilitarian objects, trees-of-life and other pieces that are halfway between fine art and fine craft – nothing has been left to chance, everything has its *raison d' etre* expressed in the captivating artistry of its living room, dining room, kitchen; in each of the family and guest bedrooms – where the children's bedroom, for example, is an invitation to recount and invent a thousand stories, to spin fables, to dream with your eyes open.

Architect Carrera continues: "In designing this house there was much emphasis placed on

two major goals: achieving really workable traffic patterns throughout the whole space and, equally important, creating a real sense of privacy while also offering endless possibilities for rejoining the social sphere. Here you can climb from the living room and terrace to enter the bedrooms on one side, then go back down to the pool and cool off: in other words, you can come and go in an ambience of privacy and conviviality. We also aimed to soften the right angles throughout most of the building with curved lines in the terrace; with faded brick cupolas, reflecting pools, fanciful *petatillo* ceramics on the ceiling, columns with rounded bases and capitals, pebble

borders, banisters simulating knotted rope, floral motifs at the entrance to the winecellar, bow windows and grand chandeliers that would widen the whole space."

Casa Eichel is a highly sensual gallery of natural panoramic views and artworks: always in balance, always displaying the sense of wellbeing, friendship and warmth upon which its interiors and exteriors are predicated, always maintaining the freshness of its original contributions to Baja Californian architecture. Without any doubt, this residence's landscape, inside and out, is proof positive of friendship, wise companionship, and love.

Casa Alcaraván

Vertical beauty

Jacinto Ávalos, Architect
Architectural Design

Ávalos Arquitectos y Asociados, SC
Construction

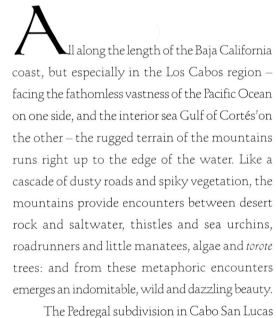

All along the length of the Baja California coast, but especially in the Los Cabos region – facing the fathomless vastness of the Pacific Ocean on one side, and the interior sea Gulf of Cortés'on the other – the rugged terrain of the mountains runs right up to the edge of the water. Like a cascade of dusty roads and spiky vegetation, the mountains provide encounters between desert rock and saltwater, thistles and sea urchins, roadrunners and little manatees, algae and *torote* trees: and from these metaphoric encounters emerges an indomitable, wild and dazzling beauty.

The Pedregal subdivision in Cabo San Lucas is a place of such encounters, at the edge of the beach where the ocean interlaces with the mountain, the dust and the breeze, the dolphin and the jackrabbit. Here we find Casa Alcaraván, a very special home because its motto might be, "Good architectural judgment begins at home." As perhaps all architects should, Jacinto Ávalos began with his own residence: this home, suspended from the clouds and rocky cliffs, is where he and his family live.

Caravan of dreams

For architect Ávalos, the design and building of this property represented a definite challenge: "Constructing this house meant putting myself under even more pressure than usual, since not only was I my own client and 'patient', but my whole family expected that my very best architectural skills would be reflected in every corner of the house. Even my father, who suffers from the same perfectionism I do, advised me to be realistic and build this to my own highest expectations, without sparing any cost, time or effort, since it was also going to be my 'calling card'."

As is almost always the case with paternal advice, Jacinto Ávalos' father was right, and his wisdom is more valid than ever. Casa Alcaraván is one of this visionary architect's very best calling cards. In his home, he's been able to put a theory and poetics of architecture to practical use. Dominion over the space, clean lines, luminousness that lets residents and objects shine, incomparable views, special care in ventilation and traffic patterns, a seriousness that bespeaks

elegance, a minimalist aesthetic, wondrous finishes on every surface, unexpected details that surprise and inspire, plays of clear and muted light, integration with the landscape, sensuality and mysticism everywhere, and an equilibrium in perpetual motion; the owner-architect's distinctive existential dynamic has been translated into an eloquent home.

One of the principal problems in building Casa Alcaraván was also one of its greatest attractions: the lot, which looks out ironically over the Pacific Ocean's mood changes, is virtually in free fall. Architect Ávalos retells his experience: "I projected this house to be built on five levels, as if it were an apartment building, because for every meter we went into the mountain, a meter of elevation was added to the proposed space. That's why my big challenge was to make it NOT seem like a five-storey building, certainly not to those of us who'd live here, nor to anyone who might visit. So I decided to group different functions vertically throughout the structure: on the lowest, the street level, I put parking and areas for services and equipment; on the second

level the pool, living and dining rooms, and kitchen; on the third level the master bedroom, a terrace, the library and my studio; on the fourth level, the children's rooms – which have the added advantage of being able to be closed off when the children aren't here – and on the fifth level, the roof and patio where my children can play, and most of all, the lawn and garden that connect directly to the mountain."

Reminiscence and desire

With its capacity for transforming itself into a vertical fountain of emotions and dreams, Casa Alcaraván – the first house built in this region – is constantly creating agreeable sensations for its residents and visitors. Not only does the pool meld with the ocean's majesty, but inside we see a staircase and a Sergio Bustamante sculpture, both consciously chosen and placed in the inner patio for their "serenity value". A blue painting converts the dining area into a great aquarium with large and small marine motifs, partitions retract into the walls, grand portholes fill the living room with light and contrasts, the lines of the terrace are seductive and shadowed. A telescope is mounted on a balcony to check what's going on with far-off boats and people, and the roof is a marvel of engineering, connecting the house with the hill so that you can almost touch the gigantic rocks and wild *damiana* flowers.

Beyond those distinguishing features, there are other functions, other details, that make this residence unforgettable. For example, its recessed niches with works of art from various eras and traditions at every staircase landing, its discreet flow of elevations, and above all its wind tower – inspired by ventilation systems for homes in Arabian desert countries. Architect Jacinto Ávalos explains: "Because we face the cliff, we couldn't give the house the kind of ventilation it'd have if it were just on the beach, with no mountain at its back. That's why it occurred to me to create a wind tower, which even has a humidifier on its top floor, for when that's

necessary. The tower has worked perfectly all along. Using it daily is like living on the hearth of a fireplace; the tower is like the chimney. For ventilation, convection, wind direction, temperature; the wind tower is a solution that works beautifully with all of Los Cabos' climactic conditions."

And a favorable wind blows upon Casa Alcaraván: all of its occupants, permanent or occasional, have been well-satisfied with architect Jacinto Ávalos' "model home". Each has fallen under the spell of this vertical caravan of aesthetics at work, of conjunctions and dysjunctions, of dreams, reminiscences, desires...

CASA KOLL

PROVENCE IN LOS CABOS

DON AND KATHI KOLL
OWNERS

ROBERT DALLAS, ARCHITECT
SAINT PAUL DE VENCE, FRANCE
PEDRO MEZA SERVÍN, ARCHITECT
SAN JOSÉ DEL CABO, MÉXICO
ARCHITECTURAL DESIGN

PEDRO MEZA SERVÍN, ARCHITECT
PROYECTO Y EDIFICACIÓN INTEGRAL, SA DE CV
CONSTRUCTION

DONALD J. ROBINSON & KATHI KOLL ASSOCIATES
INTERIOR DESIGN

GEORGE GIRVIN ASSOCIATES, INC.
GARDEN DESIGN

The traditional architecture of the south of France, and especially of that universe of light and color known as Provence, is so full of marvels that it has not only been immortalized by painters such as Van Gogh, Manet, Renoir, Cézanne, Monet, Gauguin and Picasso, but has been researched, preserved and recreated in contemporary times by architects who seek to capture its variety, distinctiveness and eternal truths – and to go beyond, transcending time and space and transferring it to other lands.

To take in Provence's wide-ranging style a pair of allusions, to two great artists, will suffice. Van Gogh wrote excitedly about southern France and its ineffable qualities: "...The land is a prairie punctuated by white and yellow flowers. Blue backdrop, a white city, and a river. All humanity, all nature, reduced to their simplest expression. It is a strange and happy encounter of bygone times with modern...Very romantic, if you like, but I would just say authentically Provençal."

For her part, art historian Marisa Vescovo describes the relationship that the genial painter Cezanne had with Provence. "Cezanne wanted to forever capture the Provençal landscape in order to eternally stop and preserve the essence of his birthplace, revealing the secrets of light in a kind of great "placenta" where he'd manage to forget anything about the place that might annoy him. Natural and manmade seem to blend into a recreation of Provence's homes, where the essential contours of the dwelling and the

mountain contribute to the parallelism and beauty of the overall composition."

Secret correspondence

Scots architect Robert Dallas is one of today's most respected specialists in the realm of Provençal aesthetics and architecture, and over the years he has intensively studied homes of various sizes and styles in the south of France. His researches have concentrated especially on the antique architecture of homes and public buildings in the town of Saint Paul de Vence, the use of materials in the region, the techniques and compositional solutions that go into the quality of the structures, their visual charm and compelling beauty.

Robert Dallas himself coordinated the architectural project to create, together with architect Pedro Meza Servín, this phenomenon facing the Sea of Cortés: a house in the pure Provençal style of Sant Paul de Vence, France, here in the heart of Los Cabos, Mexico.

Beyond some self-assured travel through space and time, stylishly placing a modern family's life amidst centuries-old rocks and mysticism at the edge of the sea, Casa Koll is the product of earnest architectural research: a building project

that was consciously designed with a good dose of charm, playfulness, creativity and imagination. The goal was to build one of the best-developed versions of Provence's distinctive architectural expression, in Los Cabos: a dwelling of light and mystery, with ample gardens and terraced patios, rooms worthy of an immortal artist and mazes in which to lose and find yourself again – as in a dream, not in the Provençal countryside but beneath the Mexican sun, and looking down upon the moist sand of Baja California's best beaches.

Provençal fire

Walking through Casa Koll we have a sense of distance and isolation, an idea that real life is going on somewhere else: clearly a result of the home's eerie feeling of antiquity. Despite its perfect juxtaposition in the Los Cabos landscape, its soul and moods evoke the time and space to which it belongs conceptually: the heterodox Provence of medieval religion, travelers following the stars, pilgrims in search of the Holy Grail. From the wide entryway complete with both Mexican and European plants, we are transported with a touch of magic and mystery into the Castle, no, forgive me, into Casa Koll: its natural stone held together

with sand-colored mortar, a very special light stone in this region where darker tones predominate; the giant roof tiles, arranged using the traditional method of dripped mortar, which were brought especially from a XIX century Veracruz hacienda; the tile floors upon which there still appear animals and fantastic symbols, from an age-old Andalucian estate; the unusual ironwork that is highlighted especially in the front door, and the torches that light the way at night, when enchantment is the home's only guiding force.

Walking through Casa Koll's different levels and rooms is like moving through a fable. The metal seagulls and stylized fireplace of the main

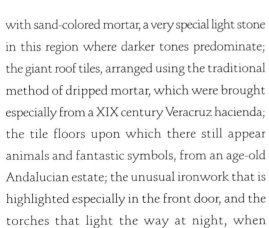

living room defy gravity; the garden paths, for their part, take marvelous twists and turns. Past a window and door that you'd never see in Saint Jean de Lux, an oven outfitted for the gastronomical style of Nice, then a group of swimming pools as luminous as Los Cabos itself, and a mural of tiles colored to reflect the immensity of Baja California.

Casa Koll is neither castle nor palace, nor a farmhouse from the palette of Cezanne or Van Gogh that has been moved willy-nilly from one continent to another. Simply and not-so-simply, it is the most exciting and inspiring Mexican beach house, with its nocturnal fire and Provençal air, in this region.

Casa Las Olas

Tropical desert

Arquitecta Lorenia Riva Palacio Delmar
Ingeniero Luis Raúl Romo Carrillo
Diseños y Construcciones DYC
Proyecto Arquitectónico y Construcción

Ticia Álvarez
Diseño de Interiores

There's a simplicity of line, shape and composition that appears at first glance upon reaching this house: contemplating it creates a pleasing impression, as when you meet someone and can immediately glimpse his or her unique essence and depth. Our first impression is confirmed and reconfirmed with a tour of its interiors and exteriors; its gardens, terraces, living rooms, bedrooms; its overall design and its smallest details.

Achieving such simplicity, free of all pretensions and false illusions, going beyond a determinate concept and style to settle itself in destiny, body, meaning and spirit, is rare. But at Casa Las Olas we feel it in all our senses — although we also feel the challenge of architecture here in a landscape whose wild vegetation and relentless heat place it somewhere between tropics and desert.

A perfect view

In all fields of life and art, simplicity needs a touch of extravagance, a bit of ambiguity, something disconcerting, that allows it to bare itself, in all its splendor, to our view. From this perspective, Casa Las Olas makes its conceptual and structural simplicity into a labyrinthine game of contrasts, a carnival of unexpected details, a to-and-fro of images and allegories without a bit of architectural ponderousness or baroque embellishment; from the street-level front door right down to the stairs that lead to the beach.

Crossing the entry gate of this residence, the first surprise is the profusion of desert and tropical plant species that have chosen to coexist throughout the property's various zones, to heighten our perceptions: the leathery green of the aloe that caresses and cures anyone who passes, the scent of jasmine and perfume of

gardenia, the elegant moves of the palm trees when they ask the *torotes* to dance, the aphrodisiac smell of the *damiana* flower ready for whenever an occasion presents itself, the timeless sighing of banana leaves rustled by the wind, and off in the distance, the landscape like a fruit so juicy it might spill down your chin.

All the prodigious simplicity of Casa Las Olas is a perfectly mounted stage-set that hides any trace of the behind-the-scenes design talent and construction work that made it a reality. Architect Lorenia Riva Palacio's principal collaborator, the engineer Luis Raúl Romo, talks about the main structural difficulties the project

presented: "This property is not on easy terrain, it was a really steep ravine facing the ocean, with a gully that ran into the sea. After the zone was developed the ravine was still here, so we had to level the land, build retaining walls and prepare a foundation, literally and figuratively, for what it is now: a kind of large traditional Mexican house, but lighter, with more contemporary responses, and with a decided feeling for and orientation towards the sea. It also has one of the best views that you can have on this bay: to the right, Punta Gorda, and to the far left, the Hotel Palmilla. Anyone who has a panorama that frames the ocean's horizon can surely be said to have a great house."

At the edge of the rocks

If perceptions and sensations in this spare and reticent dwelling are intense and far-reaching, it is due in large part to the able design of its contradictions: from the army of plants, the *palo de arco* gazebos, the slab floor and water-splashed walls at the entrance, to the earnestness of a semicircular sand-and-pebble passageway with a reflecting pool to accompany you on your way to the main living room; from the light sepia glaze on a white base that give, the façade its antique look, to the explosion of red in an armchair on the terrace closest to the sea; from the retaining wall that's been transformed into a garden facing the sea, and over which a wire is strung to keep seagulls from getting anywhere near the pool, to the rustic windows of the bedrooms, and wooden bars with arabesque latticework to encourage cross-ventilation throughout the house.

The most unexpected or trivial details make the difference in Casa Las Olas compared with other contemporary beach mansions: the stone border that goes in and out through the house, the enigmatic *torote* with its arms almost stretching over the pool which at certain hours of the day resembles nothing more than a surrealist landscape painting, the tropical vines and plants everywhere, elevating one's mood with Mexican forget-me-nots and a bouquet of scents, the large veranda for meetings and *rendezvous*, the curving stairs alongside the swimming and reflecting pools that lighten architectural volumes; open circulation throughout the house which permits freedom of movement for the adventuresome spirit, as well as precious privacy.

In front of this house the sea crashes with all its might against the rocks, the wind offers no mercy, mussing hair and tangling skirts – sometimes both. In the distance, surfers sketch their playful calligraphy onto Palmilla Bay. Inside, the house looks serene, with no stress or stridency. The tropics merge with the desert, the desert with the seemingly infinite Sea of Cortés. At the edge of the sea and the cliffs, Casa Las Olas transforms itself, with its lines and volumes, its wanderings and escapes, its backstage and opening nights, its siroccos and dreams, into a mansion of simplicity.

Casa La Playa

Space, sand and sun

Jacinto Ávalos, Architect
Remodeling Design

Ávalos Arquitectos y Asociados, SC
Construction

In Los Cabos as in any other corner of the globe, one of the many options for architecture and building is to refurbish a space which for one reason or another needs to be modified to give it renewed life – a new purpose, or a new destiny.

Casa La Playa's owners decided to remodel their residence, and contracted architect Jacinto Ávalos to design and construct an original project: "Casa La Playa was a total remodeling project. There´s no comparison between the earlier house and what is here now. The former structure was a not-very-friendly one, and it had various problems: it was a kind of maze without any real solution for maneuvering it, a dark house, poorly laid out, with only three bedrooms... it was even difficult to walk through, because of the odd decision to use a particular kind of pebbled floors. It was a house that hadn't realized its greatest potential, that needed to be reinterpreted in order to deliver maximum usefulness. Casa La Playa was a very interesting case of what it actually is to remodel something, to take a construction which from a design point of view hasn't achieved its goals, to rework it and show it to its best possible advantage."

Basking in the sun of creativity

In architect Ávalos' new project for Casa La Playa we can see the intention of opening the space to freedom and magnanimousness, to make it luminous. This completely-renovated house integrates itself to perfection with its bounteous natural surroundings on the Baja coast, where the nearly white tones of the sand make the light dance, and the Sea of Cortés' turquoise waters ebb and flow in a never-ending medley of songs.

121

Going past the entrance, where the wind plays with the newly-installed bell, and a relocated fountain murmurs a thousand stories, we can take note of all the changes in shape and depth, all the new creative tasks architect Ávalos had for this property: "I belong to a school of architecture whose concern for artistry and aesthetics is fundamental if you want to achieve a dynamic equilibrium between a space and its function. It's more like an architectural tradition, which locates itself in the natural surroundings, works with them, always respects them: a contexualist current – clean, serious, minimalist – that approaches, by various routes, the work of architects like Legorreta, Barragán and Tadao Ando. In Casa La Playa I made modifications I thought apt in terms of my tradition, deriving the best of this magnificent natural setting and highlighting it, adapting the house to the beach's own aesthetic lines."

The predominant intention surely seems to be merging with sand, sun, all the beauty of the landscape. From virtually the moment you cross the threshold, you're delighted by splendid views of the beach and the sea beyond. In fact, four bedrooms (of the six which were created in this new project) are built at beach level – allowing family and guests to watch the tide coming in

and going out. The kitchen, too, boldly located in the heart of the home, is designed for breakfasting, or dining in the afternoon, with all eyes on the ocean.

From the brushed light-toned pine woodwork to the repeated use of blinds, from the soft luminousness of the skylights to the quarry stone and travertine marble floors that seem to be a continuation of the sand, from the absence of eaves to the recurrent visual frames and points of reference, from the cross-ventilation and the wave-like curve of the arched doorways, each of the interior building elements clarifies the architectural concept that lies behind it, so that they, as well as the exterior forms, are accomplices and allies in the generation of a new spatial reality.

Sand on skin

The roof tiles were preserved, but much of the rest of Casa La Playa was brilliantly transformed: with decisive change and innovation, a room was created within a wide and functional terrace surrounding the pool, steps from the sunrooms

and barbecue, and it has become the center of social life, pleasant conviviality, fun and relaxed gatherings with family and friends.

Along with this open area for relaxation and capriciousness that faces the immeasurable beauty of the Sea of Cortés, Casa La Playa also has private corners, spaces for withdrawing into one's own thoughts, like the interior patio where the crashing of the surf becomes a faraway echo. The space offers itself to those who want to be alone without losing touch, a pause and haven in the day where time seems to stop for awhile, and one feels like a seagull who alights on a rock to take a breather, then flies off on its way.

Casa La Playa's name describes it to the letter: it is simply, or maybe not so simply, a dwelling belonging to the beach, its interior layout determined by its lovely natural surroundings.

The experience of living here is elegantly turned outwards, where there is no boundary between the dune and the house; where the light over the sea continues its journey of intensity and passion through the garden, past the pool, into the terrace, the dining room, kitchen, bedrooms; exiting in a headlong rush past the splashing fountain at the entrance.

Here in this authentic beach house, there's no other way to live than to follow the light, wander through the rooms and outdoor spaces barefoot, preferably lightly-clad, full of joy and good humor, with sand on your skin and your spirit recharged.

Casa Serena del Mar

A style all its own

M. Dean Jones, Architect
Architectural Design

Marcia Kaplan
Interior Design

Antonio Carrera, Architect
Jorge Carrera, Engineer
Grupo MCA
Construction

Casa Serena del Mar is a residence in the exclusive Palmilla development, built close to the main golf course, and it might be initially summed up in the words of M. Dean Jones, the architect who conceived the project for this home. "Casa Serena del Mar doesn't belong to any specific style, or any building method that might be located in this or that architectural 'school'. To put it most accurately, I really think I'd have to duly designate it 'Kaplan style'."

If every dwelling reflects its owners in one way or another, constituting a mirror for the personalities and aspirations of those who live in it, Casa Serena del Mar surely evokes the imaginative, purposeful and conciliatory spirit of the Kaplans as a couple, and especially the intelligence, humor, presence of mind, architectural and decorative intuition of Mrs. Marcia Kaplan. With no fear of error, we could say that from the street entrance all the way until we reach the shore, from the roofbeams to poolside, from the columns in the corridors to the paintings hung on the walls, from the light

that filters through the windows to the warmth of the domestic atmosphere inside and out, Casa Serena del Mar is no personal caprice, but her veritable dream house.

A tour of transformations

Coming upon Casa Serena del Mar and glimpsing its vertical garden, its dreamlike tile roof, its small and large shutters, its labyrinthine patterns, its light sand-colored walls, its "carpet" of stone; all of its elegant simplicity becomes an invitation to wander. Looking more closely at its lines and contours, walls and recesses, we're immediately struck by how astonishment and seductiveness have emerged as the qualities that give this house its architectural purpose, its continuity and contrasts.

Going down the gently curving staircase and feeling the breezes of the fountain and garden as they accompany us along walls and through small patios, it becomes possible to appreciate the overall uniqueness of Casa Serena del Mar: a uniqueness residing in its equilibrium and play of transitions – rites of passage between one area

and another –; in its ineffable way of reinventing itself at every turn, a continual willingness to go beyond its own limits and offer something more.

And this "something more" is inevitably a departure for the sight, smell, hearing, taste and touch; an erotic revelation, in that Casa Serena del Mar is a place where the spatial transitions are suggestive, inciting and expanding our feelings and emotions. You need only reach the bottom of the stairs and arrive in the vestibule to start feeling an urge to kick off your your shoes and walk barefoot on the cool floors of quarry stone, regional stone and travertine marble; or enter the main living room and recognize its two-tiered archway as akin to those in central Mexico's old convents, for your imagination to start making up stories. Or, sit on the comfortable terrace or under the beautifully-designed palapa with its view of the ocean, to be gripped by an uncontrollable desire: to get into the pool and swim underwater until you lose yourself, and find yourself again in the infinite line that joins the pool's water to the horizon over the sea – artifice and nature, body and soul, wind and skin, human and divine.

Living in the landscape

It should not be thought that in presenting an indefinite style, which is actually quite deliberate, Casa Serena del Mar would contain a motley assortment of timeworn and avant-garde architectural tendencies. On the contrary: this residence has the clearest intentions and objectives, which not only meet and exceed expectations, but update them day and night. To be a beach house that gets daily use, functional and comfortable; to be a home harboring plenty of surprises, open to innovations, whose two

floors and various outside areas reflect of its owners' tastes and motivations; to be an organic home where one can live and work in serenity and tranquility.

From this viewpoint, neither can Casa Serena del Mar be considered a typical Palmilla development residence, its style somewhere between Californian and Mexican. By no means would you be tempted to oversimplify and group it with the rest, whether at first glance or in your appreciation of what's behind its lines and tracery. Touring its rooms, you see that they contain nary a superfluous object nor one that hasn't been well-considered. In its kitchen,

impeccable technology meets a taste for antiquities. In the staircase leading to bedrooms on the upper floor, there hangs a beloved and very current painting, which adds vivacity to the humble act of climbing up and down; in niches throughout the house, art and artisanry coexist, crossing borders and banishing labels. And in its gardens and seaside sitting rooms, the hour of dusk is an invitation to go past superficial things and see beauties most profound.

Mrs. Kaplan is convinced that "Casa Serena del Mar is, of course, the best house in Palmilla." She says this without false modesty nor a jot of vanity, absolutely no stuffiness nor arrogance.

Instead she speaks from the conviction of one who actually lives in a house built at these heights of expectation and desire, of illusion and possibility – nothing more nor less. For her, there could be no home nicer than hers, because it's absolutely the house she yearned for, dreamed of having brought to reality someday.

From this subjective and personal perspective Casa Serena del Mar is a space with its own distinctive style where the only goal is to live in the landscape, and – above all – to reflect the vitality of the shared dream that pulses day and night under its roof, along its walls and stone floors', as it looks out over a sea of darkness and light.

Casa Alegría

The spirit of a new hacienda

Lorenia Riva Palacio Delmar, Architect
Ingeniero Luis Raúl Romo Carrillo, Engineer
Diseños y Construcciones DYC
Architectural Design y Construction

Ticia Álvarez
Interior Design

Recreating the architecture of central and western Mexico's haciendas in a coastal zone like Los Cabos, so distant from those regions and distinct from their historical and sociological context, is a building challenge that requires having in-depth knowledge of Mexican architectural history, along with creative audacity and a talent for innovation.

Architect Lorenia Riva Palacio combines the knowledge, imagination and skill needed for undertaking such a project – which is why she was able to daringly give shape to her clients' desires, building the architectural evocation of a Mexican hacienda on a medium-sized lot in Los Cabos' Palmilla community.

The result of having risen to this professional challenge is Casa Alegría, a home that evokes, as a whole and throughout each of its rooms, the Mexican hacienda architectural style which was typical of the XIX century; though with modern formal solutions to provide a residence that is functional, dynamic and contemporary, where past and present may graciously coexist.

Stones blessed by light

From the first details of the entrance, we note a lively convergence of modernity and tradition. A wrought iron gate and wooden doorway separate the street from Casa Alegría's garden, a garden which surrounds the house with grass and gardenias, ficus and bougainvilleas, banana and palm trees of all shapes and sizes.

Walking across the lawn, you can appreciate Casa Alegría's exterior from a distance: rough stone walls intersperesed with those which are lightly polished, stained in sepia tones on a white background; windows and doors of distressed wood, low stone walls of varying heights, a fountain worthy of a Jorge Negrete movie. An archway leads to the front door, its black quarry stone columns with square bases and capitals brought here from Guadalajara. The outline of the tile roof, deep ogee moldings in quarry stone, *palo de arco* branches roofing the mosaic walkway, also of quarry stone.

To the right of the entryway, before you step through the heavy double door that stands between two large stone walls, you see an open-

air breakfast room beneath a structure of woven *palo de arco* branches, set at a 45 degree angle to provide agreeable shade while you enjoy, in keeping with the décor, a meal that is *muy mexicana*. Entering Casa Alegría allows us to comprehend the challenge of building stone and light into something real: from the outside, it seems like a one-storey structure, but upon seeing its living rooms, bedrooms and terraces we realize that it is an architectural feat on two levels, which at every moment, in every corner and detail, seeks solutions that will pay homage to the whole universe that was encompassed by a traditional Mexican hacienda.

Past and present

The floor of crushed seashell mosaic, the chromatic treatment of the walls resembling an antique sepia-tone photograph, the immense ironwork chandelier and large central beam of the main living room, which symmetrically shoots wooden arrows left and right into a room so large that it accomodates dining area, sitting room and bar – these images set the tone for Casa Alegría's interiors: interiors which accentuate the evocation of an ideal Mexican hacienda, with its elements of self-assured period décor that were especially made, piece by piece, in Tlaquepaque, Jalisco.

From this perspective, passing between bedrooms and baths, through hallways, into the kitchen that connects directly to the outdoor breakfast area, looking up at the spot-lighting hung between the beams, to the rustic shutters at the windows, the ancient-looking doors; with every step we're confirming that Casa Alegría is architect Lorenia Riva Palacio's colorful interpretation of a Mexican hacienda, built in a residential community with strict building regulations and designed to comply with the clients' stipulations – which have been fully met and celebrated, in this Los Cabos version.

And who wouldn't be delighted to walk out onto the terrace and seat themselves beneath the archway separating the interior from the pool area, where you can enjoy the Sea of Cortés' freshest breezes; or walk the pebbled path until you reach the palapa of poles and palm leaves where you can sit in rustic leather and wooden *equipales*. Or, to swim beneath the Baja California sun or moonlight in the two-level pool, or listen to the small waterfuall that connects the two pools; or dine and chat *al fresco*, or discover the garden's great and small marvels, placed at different elevations around the house and leading to the back street and to the beach, a few blocks away.

Joy is a palpable presence in this house, and it's not the fictitious joy of the movies, but the perennial joy, ephemeral and eternal, of knowing that in this place the past and present interweave architectural concepts with daily reality – under a roof where, from time to time, we hear history's heartbeat, an invocation to the ancient spirit of Mexico's haciendas.

Casa Cerro

The language of the centuries

Julio López, Architect
Architectural Design and Construction

One of the geographic features of the Los Cabos region, at the southern end of the Baja California peninsula, is the appearance on the land's horizon of a mountain chain with sparse and strange vegetation, running parallel to both of its coastlines, along the Pacific Ocean and the Sea of Cortés.

Several kilometers from the Baja Californian vertex that unites the two aquatic currents, at Mexico's *finis terrae* and very near the community of Cabo San Lucas, there is a sacred mountain distinguished by huge rocks, with cactus plants dotting it from foothills to peak. Here a house has been built, and it balances most unsettlingly between the sharp rocks that scrape the clouds, and the implacable ocean waves that separate and unite the continents of Asia and America.

Inland beauty

The name of this residence with its roots sunk in the mountain and its outlook over the ocean – Casa Cerro, or Hilltop House – defines its architectural principles and motives. On the one hand, the goal was to camouflage the four-level structure with the topography of the steep windswept mountain, its giant rocks and broken lines, its *torotes* and acacias, its thistles and thorns, rampant vines and arid soil; with its gullies and *barrancas* pointing toward the Mexican Pacific, as if seeking a consummation of the long-dreamed-of union between earth and sea.

On the other hand, there was an equally vehement wish that everything in the house, from social areas to private quarters, be oriented in the direction of the ocean. From the places where family and guest bedrooms emerge from the mountain rocks, to terraces where the winds shiver and whisper, to outlook points which make meditation the greatest joy on earth, to the reflecting pools, jacuzzi and swimming pool reflecting the naked sky and sea: all should have no other aim than to mirror and multiply the primeval essence of the view.

So this dwelling with its bold, playful and suggestive lines transforms its chameleon relationship with the land and surroundings into a creative and artistic vocation, a festive play of intensity, sensation and pleasure. Such an architectural *divertissement* goes well beyond the

use of coppery ochre color on the exterior to recreate the chromatic characteristics of the region's hills, or its precise siting on the sacred mountain so that its highest and widest terrace can be found just meters from the incomparable panorama at the peak.

In reality, what is fundamental to its purpose of mimicking the landscape is the correct conceptual and practical use throughout, of geometric forms that are sinuous, curving, scalloped like the waves on the shore: cylinders, circles and semi-circles which synthesize and evoke nature's own shapes; the rocks' irregular edges, the precarious ascents and descents of the mountain, the capricious geography of this last bastion of Baja California before it reaches the confluence of the Pacific Ocean and the inland sea.

Looking beyond

In Casa Cerro time goes by irreverently and uninhibitedly, between contemplating the mountain and looking out upon the sea. No matter what activity is in progress, no matter how innocent or compromising, the earth and water will always be faithful observers of what's happening in this house whose days and nights are spent at the edge of the wind. Ocean and mountain watch, and are watched: they make their inscrutable presences felt, effect physical and spiritual transformations and are, in short, the stuff and substance of each corner of this singular dwelling.

Touring Casa Cerro's different levels, it's not necessary to count stairs, nor fix your gaze upon the proliferation of details that blend the house into its geographic context, nor cross thresholds as if you knew ahead of time what

awaited you in each room: just be open to the experience of climbing up and down clay and crystal cylinders, blithely touching the water springing from the fountains, letting the curtains in the pale sleeping quarters play with the crosswinds, enjoying the panorama to the max, from every vantage point. From the pool with its gentle temperature at midday, the dining room with its flowers and incomparable transparency at all hours; when the melancholy afternoon dew dampens bodies wherever they may be or when an inclement night on the open terrace discourages either trivial or profound conversations. The pure delight of knowing you're here with the stars

just over your head makes it easy to not say a word, because everything is conveyed by the silence, the moment and the landscape.

If Casa Cerro is a property perfectly dovetailed with its surroundings near and far, said virtue rests in the ways its architecture understands, interprets and respects the age-old dialogue between mountain and sea, the covert communication of the centuries between land mass and water. A spiralling communication, like a cylinder furrowed over time by waves and rocks, where both give and receive, concede and exchange; earth and moisture continuing life's recurrent circle.

The *Cerro Sin Nombre*, Hill Without a Name, and the Pacific Ocean face each other, arms outstretched to show their sharp or rolling undulations: between them is only this house, which tries to replicate the natural landscape and invites us, quite insistently, to go beyond the limits of interior and exterior spaces; to see far past the easy metaphor of the walls' straight lines and the defiant curves of its secret heart.

Casa La Cascada

Continuing the rhythm of the water

Burdge & Associates
Original Architectural Design

Próspero Tapia Hernández, Architect
Consultant

Tapia Architects
Architectural Expansion Design

Protip, Design & Construction
Construction

Casa La Cascada, true to its origins in the intermittent fall of water upon the wild diversity of the land, never ceases to amaze: throughout the long course of its history it has reinvented itself, and it continues to be one of the most innovative, purposeful and daring homes in Los Cabos.

In spite of the magnificent view it has over the Sea of Cortés, very near where it joins the waters of the Pacific Ocean, this home turns our gaze inevitably inward so that we momentarily forget the natural beauties of Baja California Sur – preferring to contemplate this structure, clearly attuned to its natural surroundings but with human guidance that has culminated in an architectural project where the endless liquid murmur of a waterfall creates intervals and pauses, tempos and rhythms.

Water and rocks

Even before entering Casa La Cascada's front gate, with its stylized birds-of-paradise in shades of green, we hear water gurgling upon stones: we're spellbound by its aquatic essence and by the cleverness of flowering plants as they truly become, at least for an instant, the fantasy of a tropical Eden. In this residence with its subtle Oriental style and long history of conceptual and practical innovation, where customize arches are born from rock and the main staircase is a vertical complement to the waterfall's capricious undulations, what is startling is that an addition has been undertaken to blend perfectly with the original design; supporting bold natural and manmade solutions which give new value to the creativity and the multiplicity that have gone into this singular home.

Architect Próspero Tapia defines the characteristics of the building and its addition: "This is an expanded design which permits the original plan to flow, and allows for problem-free continuity. The challenge here was to satisfy the owners' requirements, as they wanted immediate access to the beach, which would also permit communication between the two projects, the new and the earlier construction; but done in such an integral way that it would give you no idea there'd been any addition or remodeling. In other words, they wanted the new areas (office, master bedroom, gym, slide and beach access) to be integrated, with vertical communication as well. That was resolved with an elevator that takes you down to the beach from the street-level entrance."

If the backbone of the original design is the waterfall, along which flows a major work of landscape architecture and spreading out from which the interior and exterior areas are arranged for conviviality and privacy – offering independence and isolation without creating any sense of confinement –; this new addition has managed to let a touch of Oriental style flow into its construction and spatial quality, and has added

other touches to "defy gravity"; giving the space a good dose of humor, irony, and lightheartedness. Some of Casa La Cascada's newfound touches are: a waterslide that uses other means and materials to extend the waterfall's stone trough so that it provides a fun-filled slide ending just a few centimeters from an all-welcoming pool; a gymnasium for building muscles while delighting your eye with a view of the new pool and of the sea, with each breath recalling the motto "healthy mind in healthy body"; finally, a tunnel decorated with roof and wall murals whose subjects relate to the Sea of Cortés and its many legends – a tunnel that can be reached only by an elevator which, when it reaches its last stop, opens its metal doors to bring you directly to the beach.

The floor up above

Architect Tapia alludes to problems that had to be overcome in order to create an addition that would lighten and enliven Casa La Cascada: "The region's topography was the main enemy in this building project; we had to dig down deep into the earth and at the same time provide platforms that would have the same features as those which were already there. In other words, while complying with the Palmilla residential community's building regulations, we wanted to adapt the existing Oriental influence so we'd have a play of volumes that would allow us to open the space for our various purposes: installing an elevator, creating access for golf carts, building the slide, the gym, the tunnel that connects the sea with the heights and, overseeing both the landscape and the house, the office.

While the water continues to cascade, murmuring of days gone by, this addition has

thoroughly fullfilled its objective: there is no break with the initial plan, with the first architectural design. The new version blends beautifully with the many folding doors that allow one to widen or limit privacy or sociability, with interior and exterior floors of Yucatecan marble that serve as invisible boundaries to mark the conceptual shift between one room and another, with landscaping framed by profuse vegetation and rocks here and there to remind us that the waterfall is also a cliff; with open-air showers, with bedrooms, with reflecting pools surrounding the residence amidst clouds, *damiana* flowers and palm trees.

In this addition, perhaps the most significant room, not for its spectacular or daring effect but for its sense of restraint and retreat, is the office or study. This serious, elegant, and contemporary room can be directly accessed from the hallway, after traversing a kind of isolated sanctuary. From the main office one can work the house's electronic controls, and be in communication with the rest of the world; can sit or stand to contemplate the very best views over the Sea of Cortés, and take care of business while listening to the waterfall in the foreground and the splashing of the waves in the background. Nothing could come closer to paradise than being in this space where it is also possible to work, reflect, write, plan and dream.

Meeting the sea

Thus, just as it is possible to go directly, nonstop, from the center of this new addition down to the sea – having taken the elevator or the tunnel of marvels – you may also walk down to the shore by the old stairway, with its wooden bridge almost at a level with the waterfall; or by new flagstone paths that lead via unsuspected twists

Casa del Alma

Private mysticism

Tapia Architects
Architectural Design

Protip, Design & Construction
Construction

The journey into the desert is experienced, according to Western cosmogony, as a second baptism. Trial by fire and clarity: conquering temptations, visions, shadows, appearances in order to enter the spirit realm. Nothing is more dangerous than entering the desert without a guide, but from another vital analytical perspective, nothing is more uplifting than making the desert into a dwelling for the soul.

Like any desert, the arid lands that surround Los Cabos and continue along the length of the Baja California peninsula, with pleasant oases here and there, are a spiritual place; mirrored in the watery "deserts" of the Sea of Cortés and Pacific Ocean. The border between dust and moisture dissolves: southern Baja California towns and cities are a pause, an interruption, between the two deserts that resist returning as breeze, fog

and dew. Instead, they shape an urban settlement like Los Cabos, where their souls wander with or without any sense; seeking a place, a shelter, a home.

A sacred place

From this viewpoint, an estate near the deserts, water and sand of Baja California Sur that takes Casa del Alma as its name should take on a form so special that it alludes – at least in a kind of divine irony or mystic vision – to a home for the spirit. That is indeed the case in this residence designed by architect Próspero Tapia in the Rancho Paraíso residential community, which has risen on one of the sere hills facing the Gulf of Cortés.

Casa del Alma has three cupolas of various sizes, whose straight and curved lines harmonize with and crown the hallway, the fireplace area and the kitchen. This trio gives it a sense of being

a boat about to set sail. Somewhere between Mediterranean and Andalucian in architectural style, the house also shares certain reminiscences of the outlines and façades of northern Mexico's haciendas and missions.

Entering Casa del Alma, having crossed the mystic circle of its hallway, one finds a space ruled by its wide-ranging expectations: the comfortable arrangement of its sitting areas and passageways,

the vaulted cavern of the kitchen, the intrinsic equilibrium of a dwelling destined to have its doors open while still offering its residents private corners, solitude and contemplation of the panorama that balances between desert, sea and sky.

The large living room is the axis about which scenes of daily life and its activities revolve: observatory, terrace, lounge, gameroom; places

for endless conversations as well as quiet moments; entrance zone, transit area, doorway and passageway; spaces for encounters and reveries.

Dissolving borders

Architect Próspero Tapia is clear and direct: "Our objective in Casa del Alma was to bring desert and sea together, to play with volumes and offer new sensations. It is an architectural proposal that has spirit: because of its incomparable light, panoramic view, its incessant play of colors and textures, its residents and their visitors can all feel at home here."

Few other elegant Los Cabos houses transmit such a feeling of spatial freedom – "the spirit of place transfigured in a human creation". From its architectural heart outward, this is a place where lines disperse and dissolve – lines between intellectual and sensory, between ocean and desert, between night and day, between light and darkness, between natural and manmade, between sacred and profane.

In Casa del Alma space shapes itself to organic elements in such a way that they are always present in "high volume"; that is to say, spatial priorities move outward, toward desert

plants, cactus, *torotes*, bougainvilleas; an almost pictorial impulse encompasses centuries of nature, and all of its colors.

One corner of Casa del Alma stands out for its serene flow of time and space: the terrace, roofed by a pergola of rustic poles and *palo de arco* branches: shade and sunlight, plants left and right, natural ventilation, a reflecting pool that humidifies while refreshing thoughts and sensations. Casa del Alma is a poem within a poem – everything flows in a natural way here, and

nothing is forced. Mysticism is its second skin, beneath tile and stone.

You feel this most if you gaze over the landscape toward the immeasurable blue and green grandeur of the sea.

A bird sings: the house reveals its essence, which confronts, challenges and inspires those who live and visit here. To know it is a joy, a passage in the desert: at the moment before dawn or in a private twilight, a message from what is deepest in the spirit.

Villa Puerta al Mar

A dialogue of essences

Arturo Cuevas Ledesma, Architect
Architectural Design

Alejandro Treviño Angulo, Architect
Construction

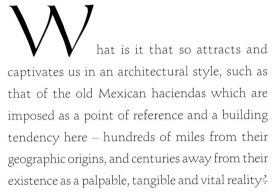

What is it that so attracts and captivates us in an architectural style, such as that of the old Mexican haciendas which are imposed as a point of reference and a building tendency here – hundreds of miles from their geographic origins, and centuries away from their existence as a palpable, tangible and vital reality?

What kind of sense does it make to reproduce, and attempt to recreate – with countless adjustments for contemporary needs and the functioning of a beachside house – all the structure and layout, the hearth and corridors, patios and rough terrain, ceilings and floors of a typical western Mexican hacienda – in Los Cabos, Baja California Sur?

Maybe the only answer, going beyond the realm of the highly subjective taste of anyone who decides to build a house with such architectural and interior design characteristics, rests in the immense capacity the word "hacienda" has for evoking images, for rediscovering lost time. This is a home whose structural qualities are as earnestly and lovingly shaped as the irrefutable and typical style of haciendas in Mexico's "old west": transparency and melancholy, evocation and truth, a soul seeking embodiment in the light and stone of Los Cabos; a XIX century mansion on the plains transported to the mountains and the sea.

Return to the old house

From this perspective, one may attempt to understand and value the project of building a house at Baja California's *finis terrae* with all the flavor of the venerable haciendas of Jalisco and environs: not to build a stage-set from nostalgia, but to truly recreate and interpret a space with precise references to a determined style and period, for contemporary lives.

Such a job of aesthetic research and design was complemented with the excellent construction of Alejandro Treviño. From the entrance to the stairs down to the beach, he has created a reality that goes significantly beyond simply complying

with the stylistic expectations of Casa Puerta al Mar's owners.

Facing one of the most imposing cliffs of Punta Ballena, on a beach that caresses and scratches with restless fingers at the Sea of Cortés, is a home that encourages us to go back in time – to the days of the *chinacos*, those brave Mexican rough riders. We hear chains clanking on wooden doors to gain entry late at night, coachmen cracking their whips, the clip-clop of horses wearily pulling carriages through huge stable gates. We peek through the smoke of waxen candles and oil lamps into a room, and spy a furtive romance going on at the barred window. Or, we're serenaded in the moonlight by the ghost of movie idol Jorge Negrete: in this setting, it's not all that difficult to recapture the lusty contradictions of Western Mexico's old haciendas.

In Puerta al Mar, we glimpse evocative images everywhere, each with its compelling ability to suggest other images, other voices, other realities. If a lone *torote* receives you with aplomb and elegance at the entrance to the house, reminding you that this land is part of Baja California's deserts and oases, it is immediately followed by an iron bell on the wall, in the best style of Guanajuato's old haciendas – right beside a door that actually came from an old hacienda. And that's even before mentioning the roof tiles laid one atop the next, their grout spilling out

through cracks; the watchtower with its skylight; the stone moldings and gargoyles, or the door that still resonates with the striking of the chains that gave it its form and character.

Flowing through time

Architect Treviño sums up the experience of entering and walking through Puerta al Mar: "Every corner in this house has been thoroughly considered. It was a real investigation into Mexican roots, especially for an architect and builder whose feet are firmly planted in the contemporary age. The challenge was that the house should look like an actual old house, and not like a new one made to look old. From the moment you arrive at big front door and then walk through it, something happens: you find yourself back in the time of the haciendas, without having ever left the present day. Reaching the privacy of the patio, your response to the house is transformed even further, and after that you understand and assimilate everything more easily: the main living room, the bedrooms, the terrace area, the spectacular view. Here, the important thing is to let yourself be carried along by the space: the way it takes history seriously, but also has a lot of imagination – and a little whimsy."

Puerta al Mar is a house where past and present coexist rather fluidly, hacienda architecture and contemporary interior design together evoking what might be thought of as typical Mexican style: popular art and artisanry, photographs of Emiliano Zapata and Frida Kahlo, oil lamps converted to electricity, a painting of San Pascual Bailón in the kitchen, a fountain in the patio – whose columns allow us to imagine that an old-time horsedrawn carriage might pull

up at any minute. Earthen color on the walls, *maguey* cactus scattered everywhere, stone flooring etched with the symbols of old branding-irons, a brick vaulted ceiling, mural and tiles with floral motifs, Saltillo-style adobe, columns from Guadalajara: fragments, vestiges, celebrations from another time and place. We can scarcely believe it when, on the other hand, the exterior terrace tempts us with a modern freeform pool, the oxidized grillwork and curving lines of the pergola and palapa relieving the property's otherwise rectilinear forms; and beyond, nearly hidden by plant-covered walls, we discover the Sea of Cortés fighting a duel to the death with the rocks of the Baja California shore.

To throw open the gates of this house is to enter another universe, old-world but dynamically attuned to our own day and age. Essences from the past and present enter into a dialogue that seek answers for creating an irresistable and habitable reality. This is why Puerta al Mar is a home that is also a bridge: leading us not only along paths through watery valleys, but into a whirlwind of convincing solutions for continuity, where today's everyday sounds meet the ballads of days gone by.

CASA HEATHER

A CONCEPT OF *MEXICANIDAD*

JACINTO ÁVALOS, ARCHITECT
REMODELING DESIGN

ÁVALOS ARQUITECTOS Y ASOCIADOS, SC
CONSTRUCTION

KATHY HOLT, DECORATOR
SALT LAKE CITY, UTAH
HEATHER HAMBY, CO-DECORATOR
INTERIOR DESIGN

Cabo San Lucas and San José del Cabo, with their natural and manmade corridors bound for Todos Santos and La Paz, comprise a whole region where, over the past several years, there have sprung up various architectural interpretations of what it is to live in Mexico. Some claim to present the essence and material form of those myriad realities and aspirations known as *mexicanidad*, "mexican-ness": faces and masks that are actually just explorations, approximations of an ideal; fantasies, images and visions with aesthetic intent.

From the time tourism and infrastructure began to be developed in Los Cabos, construction also started on a series of residences, owned by Mexicans as well as foreigners, with various agendas – but all wishing to embody the soul of Mexican style between walls and gardens, ceilings and floors, patios and terraces, secret hideaways and bright solaria. Such is the rubric which circumscribes Casa Heather's dynamism and dreams.

Transparencies

In the architectural project for this small home, neither a feeling of theoretical nor practical "authority" was sought; but rather a proposal for taking the best of what had historically been designed in Los Cabos to give each of its rooms a lively layout, and a highly visual sense of Mexican style.

The goal was quite simple: the most pleasant possible place for getting together with family, a few meters from the beach: nothing more nor less.

Perhaps because of its lighthearted expectations, Casa Heather eschews any architectural lines – especially in its interiors –

that go beyond the strictly functional. All its rooms, its dining and sitting areas and bedrooms, are simply pleased with themselves and the way they interconnect for an agreeable, warm and hospitable feeling.

However, this feeling is not due to an architectural proposal that captivates with shapes and masses, unusual solutions and quirky appearances.

The spaces encourage one to spend more time outside than in, to live beneath Baja California's sun and moon, to be fully enthralled by a sense of transcience, of memorable but fleeting instants.

Still, Casa Heather is clear with itself and others: it just offers what it has and what it is architecturally, without getting into any overwhelming spatial pretensions. From this perspective, leaving the house and jumping into the pool, spending a while under the palapa or in the terrace, becomes one of the very best options. A house for passing through: sensually open, devoted as a seagull to the outdoors, the fresh air, and the beach.

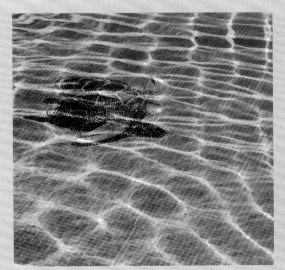

Profuse decoration

There's no doubt that Casa Heather is unique for various reasons, but one in particular is crucial for a more vivid, in-depth understanding. Beyond the turtle perched at the pool, or the palm trees that dance with the gardenias beside the palapa, what is most distinctive is seeing such profuse decoration in a space as small as this: decoration that is never tempted to contemplate the void, and which literally exudes a breath of *mexicanidad* on every inch of its walls, and throughout its flower-bedecked hallways.

The reproduction of a Frida Kahlo painting, the bold presence of *equipales* – handcrafted wooden-slat and leather furniture – and of elevated seating, the touches of clay and tin artisanry, the woven rattan of an ever-patient bench, the flowered mirrors and ceiling fixtures, sunflowers as a great aesthetic horizon in a private bedroom, the intensity of small regional details that convert themselves into an entire design concept..., all aiming to shape Casa Heather's style into a path toward what is authentic in this country, what is worth seeing reflected in a beach house set on Mexican soil.

On that point, this worthy dwelling called Casa Heather confirms its clearest motive, its essential aspiration to be nothing more than what it is. A little architectural intensity, a lot of decoration, and a continual homage to a vision of Mexico and *mexicanidad*, it opens itself to other lively possibilities: like turning the doorknob, going through the door day or night, and touching the sand of the coast to dazzle oneself with the Moon and Sun.

Casa de Luz

Poised with outspread wings

Graham and Christienne Weston
Owners

Antonio Carrera, Architect
Jorge Carrera, Engineer
Grupo MCA
Architectural Design and Construction

Christienne Weston, Design
Interior Design

In any part of the world, to live geographically speaking "on the edge", in one of those places which depending on your point of view and definition might be the end or the beginning of the known and habitable world, is an experience that over the centuries and in different cultures has ever been linked with exile, self-containment, courage and physical and psychic strength for facing the unknown; but also with serenity, poise, adaptability, and above all, liberty.

Although nowadays many things – uses, customs, landscapes, material arrangements and even social and geopolitical compositions, have changed; the edges of the world remain faithful to their ancestral nature and continue to demand an effort, 101%, of anyone who plans to live on the last frontier between earth and sea. From this viewpoint, designing and building a huge house beside the Cerro del Faro, Lighthouse Hill, right near Cabo Falso which is the true Land's

End of Baja California Sur and thus of Mexico – where there is nothing besides land and view, only the unfathomable presence of the largest ocean on the planet – requires a high level of creativity, imagination, consciousness, commitment and playfulness: such as that shown day in and day out, night after night, by the warm and pleasurable realities of Casa de Luz.

To the lighthouse

This residence at the edge of Mexico's territory, with its long two-level façade, reminds us – especially at twilight, at the instant when darkness begins to overtake the horizon, and in a thoroughly fortuitous and involuntary way – of the *finis terrae* Lighthouse on the west coast of Galicia, Spain, the original *finis terrae* where the Celts, Romans and other pilgrims to Santiago de Compostela worshipped the Sun, the mist, the powers that live between light and darkness, and

a universe that keeps its mysteries thinly veiled. Without any tinge of esoterica, though with all the enigmas borne of standing beside a Lighthouse at the end of the Baja peninsula, Casa de Luz emerges from the cliffs and sand with seductive paleness, a string of pearls on a captivating neck, a halo of eroticism that incites and excites everything from the garden's fresh greenery to the diaphonous lace in its bedrooms, and appears here and there, inside and out, with little provocation.

Poised, wings spread, ready to take a flight of calm passion and quiet enthusiasm: on this estate, the gardens are a green bridge (wide esplanades, flowerboxes at various levels, nopal cactus and gardenias gracing stone altars) between the superfine beach sand, seaside rocks of all sizes, shrubbery along the bottom of retaining walls, and quarry stone columns with gates separating private from public. And, between the pool shaped like a waterfall with three niches for resting, the cosmic circles of water and fire in the jacuzzi and fireplace pit, the open air living room that brings friends closer together amidst nature's miracles, the salt smell of the sea, bodies bathed in light, sounds of seagulls and pelicans, and opposing winds morning, noon and night.

Transubstantiations
In Casa de Luz water flows generously, abundantly and is renewed, like drops of time poured from

falgon to chalice. Vertical and horizontal reflecting pools – concave, convex – reproduce themselves in patios, hallways, and terraces.

Several quarry stone lions dispense the water that sings its welcome in the entryway, accentuating a pair of walls that smile moistly to each side while the visitor makes this aquatic rite of passage. After traveling across the marble floor in the living room and the dining room with its wicker furniture, you can follow a straight line – with no change of materials, just floor-levels – to the sea; although it's recommended you let the swimming pools divert you on your way, so you can swim down, all the way to the jacuzzi without leaving the water.

With Franciscan mission-style architecture and touches of California beach house – though it doesn't fail to use reddish tiles and blue cupolas to reflect the celestial vault of the sky – Casa de Luz has, in its large and varied rooms on the first and second floors, some of the loveliest panoramic views in all of Los Cabos. Through some windows, behind bare columns, there appears the savage and unforgiving beauty of the Pacific; in other windows, doors and skylights the ancient minimalist charm of the Cerro del Faro, Lighthouse Hill, rises with its promise of guiding our vision – and the ships that skim the coast – so that neither goes over the edge.

An innocent eroticism drapes its mantle over this house day and night, radiating like a cascade of light, inviting one to live, trust oneself, wear life like a loose garment and assimilate all the changes and signs of the times at this land's end – with equanimity, mirth, reverence and, above all, a soaring freedom.

Casa El Rincón del Sol

Mysticism and ecology

Carlos Montero
Architectural Design and Construction

From the time construction began on this house close to Cabo Pulmo, mystic energy also made its appearance, as a truth born in its very heart. Architect Carlos Montero held a ceremony whose object was to request the land's permission to build upon it, and in the exact center of the property he laid the first stone, Roman-style, and a scroll with the residents' names; then tossed corn kernels onto the ground in the age-old Mexican tradition of asking forgiveness in advance for the earth-moving to come – and also to plead for generosity, abundance and good treatment by the spirits-of-place.

And it seems those petitions were heard and favorably answered: today El Rincón del Sol is a fabulous home in every sense of the word, where one breathes an air of peace and tranquility, an energy that imbues one with serenity and passion – in colloquial terms, there are "good vibes" here –; and all through the day and night feels a spirit of reciprocity and connection with the sea and the desert.

Ecological invocations

At El Rincón del Sol, mystical invocations to the four winds and asking the land's acceptance are not empty words, not vain speeches nor the sort of "good intentions" which pave the path to a hell of contradictory declarations and actions.

The formula for translating good wishes into avant-garde architecture consisted, surely, in creating El Rincón del Sol as an environmentally-friendly home; making it the property it is today, where daily life avails itself of the sun's energy, where water-use is safeguarded, trash is recycled, the winds' rhythms are harnessed to cool the rooms and the employment of building materials is always appropriate, relevant and remarkable. The home's owner once made a comment to architect Montero, and these words became the key and linchpin for the construction of El Rincón del Sol: "I have a dune facing the Sea of Cortés, and I'm yearning to build a house there, but at the same time I absolutely want to preserve nature, not to offend it."

Given that perspective, having won the bid for the work and identifying completely with the owners' goals and dreams, the architect threw himself into the job of making El Rincón del Sol a reality: little by little the home emerged among the dunes, mimicking their shapes in its walls and curving lines, using adobe as a the basic wall material (which keeps rooms cooler), finding the tone of paint most similar to that of the sand dunes then using it on the plaster of the interiors and matching it with the grain of the marble in the exterior finishes.

The result of this adventure is a design that is architecturally well-developed, in that nature's moods have been respected to the letter, and integration with the landscape is not a fashionable concept but a palpable reality and existential creed; where the desert vegetation unique to this region is reflected in responses throughout the length and breadth of the house, where the sea is not just a lovely panoramic view in a protected environmental zone but, once it has been desalinized, the principal source of water used in the home.

Spatial mysticism

If the natural undulations of the dunes are a reflection of the architectural lines in El Rincón del Sol's façade and exteriors, so are the desert plants and flowers as they wend their way towards the sea, almost as if the house didn't exist. Perhaps the passageways and patios, the

interiors, the pool and the brief parentheses of the lawn areas, are resting places which have been approved by the environment, by the desert spirits who night and day careen toward the edge of the jade- and turquoise-tinged sea.

After entering through a heavy well-guarded gate, you hardly register the moment at which you've entered the property. The rough road between cactus and *torote* plants seems to go on and on, but after a few curves in the road the first palms, agave cactus and tropical flowers appear.

Like a mirage in the desert, El Rincón del Sol also comes into view for the first time, its two levels in an infinite play of rounded and serpentine lines which seem carved by the wind and the sand. A wall with a circle broached by *torote* limbs receives visitors. The driveway is a great circle intersected by three palm trees, which now and then try to touch the seagulls soaring among the clouds above.

From our first contact with this home, nature reminds us that it has been here since time primordial, that it is the protagonist in this story of the meeting between sea and desert. The house respects this, and its rooms themselves

seem to be mystical in the way they unfold. Perhaps this is why the curving walls seem to be aching for a caress, the plants and flowers seem disposed to overhear private thoughts, the flagstones and marble floors watch your every step, and the doors open themselves to the flow of air and energy.

Symbiosis with the World

But with all this mysticism it should not be thought that El Rincón del Sol is a place to retire from the world, a kind of monastery at Land's End: to the contrary, it is a residence whose ecological vision accomodates a tennis court and airy circular showers, and it offers places for stretching out, having fun, engaging in convivial conversation, physical and spiritual relaxation.

You need only cross the threshold into the hallway where a high-relief copper sculpture depicts suns and moons (created by the same fine artisan from Santa Clara del Cobre, Michoacán who made the flowerpots and lamps for the entire house), to arrive at a vestibule which is a veritable crossroads for the breezes and beauty

of Baja California's waters. To the right, the social area with its living room, dining room and kitchen. To the left, the bedrooms and guestrooms. On both sides, a stained glass panel framing an exquisite installation by conceptual artist Víctor Guzmán, evoking a rain of clear sounds over a sea of sand and conch shells.

Inside, the walls do not follow the the exterior curves; instead, their flat rectilinear lines suggest greater privacy and warmth, though they do not eschew circles entirely. These appear in the ceiling, where light dances and the hours whisper through the day.

The height of these rooms allows for operation of two heat-exchangers, located in each of the house's main zones, which absorb and expel warm air in order to give a constant feeling of coolness in the hot season: during the rare cold spells, both exchangers adapt to produce an opposite, warming effect for the home.

Face to face with the sea, El Rincón del Sol softens and shades itself like the curving dunes which mold themselves to the Gulf's implacable waves. Its terraces and palapas are open to restfulness or mischief, to games, meditations, private or everyday conversations with no other eavesdroppers than the manta rays, flying fish and pelicans who trace their paths through the air and water.

Authentic in its body and soul, its wishes and dreams, El Rincón del Sol is a home where time sprinkles itself upon the sand tangled in tree roots, and individual energies are recharged by life's own positive energy – flowing along sinuous and rounded lines, closing and opening to reveal the flowering of true ecology, of mystic union with the world.

DIRECTORY

ARQUITECTO JACINTO ÁVALOS
AVALOS ARQUITECTOS Y ASOCIADOS
www.avalosarquitectos.com
javalos@avalosarquitectos.com

ARQUITECTO ANTONIO CARRERA
INGENIERO JORGE CARRERA
GRUPO MCA
www.grupomca.com
acarrera@grupomca.com

ARQUITECTO ROBERTO CONTRERAS SANDOVAL
ARKCO
www.arkcoarq.com
rcontreras@arkcoarq.com

ARQUITECTO M. DEAN JONES
www.deanjonesarchitect.com
www.architectcabo.com
architectmdj@earthlink.net

DISEÑADORA EMMA LAURA DÍAZ SANTANA RÁBAGO
kinydi@prodigy.net.mx

ARQUITECTO JULIO LÓPEZ
cabogrupo@prodigy.net.mx

CARLOS MONTERO
www.montero-architects.com
arquitectos@montero-architects.com

ARQUITECTO PRÓSPERO TAPIA HERNÁNDEZ
www.tapiaarchitects.com
prosperotapia@tapiaarchitects.com

ARQUITECTO JAIME ORTEGA ARNAIZ
HOMES AT CABO, S.C.
joarnaiz@prodigy.net.mx

ARQUITECTO PEDRO MEZA SERVÍN
PROYECTO Y EDIFICACIÓN INTEGRAL, SA DE CV
www.pyeisa.com.mx
pyeisa@prodigy.net.mx

ARQUITECTA LORENIA RIVA PALACIO DELMAR
INGENIERO LUIS RAÚL ROMO CARRILLO
DISEÑOS Y CONSTRUCCIONES DYC
www.dycphotos.com
lorenia@rivapalacio.com

ARQUITECTO ALEJANDRO TREVIÑO ANGULO
www.atatreviño.com
ata_alejandro@prodigy.net.mx